CLIFF RICHARD

THE COMPLETE RECORDING SESSIONS

1958-1990

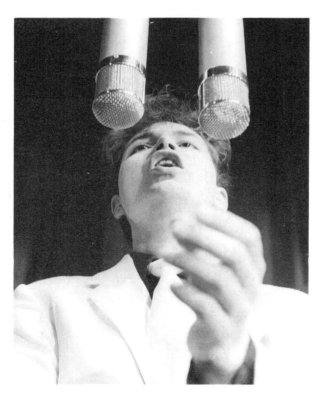

CLIFF RICHARD

THE COMPLETE RECORDING SESSIONS

1958-1990

PETER LEWRY AND NIGEL GOODALL

FOREWORD BY CLIFF RICHARD

BLANDFORD

This book is dedicated
to our wives
Carole and Marylyn
whose support and encouragement
made it possible

Blandford
An imprint of Cassell,
Villiers House, 41–47 Strand, London WC2N 5JE

First published in the UK 1991

Distributed in the United States by
Sterling Publishing Co., Inc.
387 Park Avenue South, New York, N.Y. 10016–8810

Distributed in Australia by
Capricorn Link (Australia) Pty Ltd
P.O. Box 665, Lane Cove, NSW 2066

British Library Cataloguing in Publication Data
Lewry, Peter *1956–*
    Cliff Richard: the recording sessions 1958–1990.
    1. Pop music. Richard, Cliff
    I. Title   II. Goodall, Nigel *1950–*
    781.64092

ISBN 0–7137–2242–8

Printed and bound in Great Britain
by The Bath Press

Contents

Preface

The central issue of this book is the body of recordings made by Cliff Richard. This, we hope, will be the definitive work for those who really want to know the 'ins and outs' of the music, as recorded by Cliff.

We have attempted to present the complete facts concerning what exists on tape. Unfortunately, there are many unresolved questions upon which this book cannot throw light. It is unclear whether film company vaults may or may not contain extra songs from the movies as well as original recording tapes.

Although some tapes were thrown out by EMI in 1966, we have documented the alternative and unissued takes as accurately as possible.

This book will discuss all known and released Cliff Richard recordings, as well as the many rare items known to exist. We have tracked down as much information as possible on each and every record and recording, and pieced it together in order to present a clear and detailed analysis of Cliff's music.

PL & NG

Foreword

It would never have crossed my mind to dig through mountains of studio archives for dusty old track listings and details of long-forgotten recording sessions. Maybe I've a legitimate excuse, in that I'm just too busy touring and adding today's recording to yesterday's lists. The truth is, of course, that I'd never have the patience to thumb through one file, let alone hundreds!

Happily, there are those who believe our musical past – or some of it – is worth preserving and sharing, and are prepared to invest effort to ensure that it happens. I doff my hat to Nigel and Peter, who are two such guys, and I'm flattered, to say the least, that it's my work they've chosen to research.

Recording, of course, has been the cornerstone of my career and that, together with performing, still is the great love of my life. For me, a recording project has never been an end in itself, but rather the start of a creative process. The studio environment sets me thinking, not only about the immediate sounds we want to achieve, but how I'll eventually perform the material on stage or on TV. I even find myself working out lighting effects and choreography potential!

I pride myself on working well in a studio – mainly, I suppose, because time is usually unpressurised. No one calls to distract or interrupt and, although I work fast compared to many artists, an album usually takes at least two or three months. I love the luxury of having no deadlines. If we don't finish something today, then, no matter, there's always more time tomorrow if necessary. As I say, though, I'm not one for hanging round nattering or doing nothing. Studio time is money – big money these days – and I don't waste it.

Technically, of course, I can't begin to relate to today's computerised magic. I have a kind of awed respect for the engineers who give the impression of such total and nonchalant control. I don't have a clue how it all works. I just know that, if I want the impossible, all I have to do is ask! That's why I've no inclination whatsoever to turn back the clock. In the 'old' days, making a good record was largely dependent on the arrangement, and that was completed before ever setting foot in the studio. All musicians had to do was play their dots, the vocalist had to sing in tune, and the engineers had to get the balance right. Today, record making is about inspired and often spontaneous production and musicianship, and the apparently endless choice of sounds and effects makes it a tremendously rewarding and stimulating experience.

If we're talking nostalgia, then there's no doubt that EMI's internationally famous studios in Abbey Road, London, hold most memories. The early stuff that the Shads and I largely improvised, and the wise and patient advice of our fondly-remembered producer, Norrie Paramor, seemed to occupy a whole era. As you'll realise from what follows, however, I've worked at many different studios over the years and, to be truthful, I'm not specially committed to any one. Obviously some studios are better equipped than others, but then you can always hire in bits of specialised equipment if required. For me it's people that matter more than places and, if the technicians, engineers, musicians and producers are good at their jobs, and if the creative vibes are good, then little else matters. A sobering fact disclosed by the book, that may disappoint or delight according to taste, is that there's precious little unissued and unheard material of mine stashed away in studio vaults. On my demise, at least no one will be able to cash in with a flood of hitherto unreleased material!

Thanks then to Nigel and Peter for an amazing piece of work. You've stirred my memory right enough, and made a unique contribution to the industry by bringing together what, in all modesty, surely has to be a bit of UK pop history.

Cliff Richard

Acknowledgements

We would like to thank the following people for their assistance and endeavours in helping us with this book:

Bill Latham, David Bryce, Malcolm Smith, Roger Bruce, Peter Gormley, Gill Snow and all at the Cliff Richard Organisation; Terri Anderson; Ken Townsend, Lou Swoffer, Richard Lee and Peter Vince at EMI Abbey Road Studios; Ruth Edge and Jenny Keen at EMI Music Archives, Hayes; Jill Betts, Amanda Rabbs and Matt Duffy at EMI Manchester Square; Bruce Welch, Mike Read, Ashley Howe and Tony Clark; Paul Moessl;

Gerry Kitchingham and Ben Robbins at RG Jones Studios; Stock, Aitken and Waterman at PWL; Mayfair Studios; Air Studios; Sarm Studios; Mike Gardner at Eden Studios; Gerry Bron at Roundhouse Recording Studios; Keith Bessey and Stuart Colman; See for Miles Records and John Waller at Polydor Records; Steve Maycock at Sotheby's; Graham Cossins, Peter Day, Keith Allfrey, Christine Whitehead and Harry de Louw.

. . . and very special thanks to Cliff Richard.

Photo Credits

Every effort has been made to correctly acknowledge the source and/or copyright holder of each illustration, and the publisher apologises for any unintentional errors or omissions, which will be corrected in future editions of this book.

David Bryce 129; Comic Relief/WEA 134; Paul Cox/The Cliff Richard Organisation 8; Andy Earl/EMI 2; Marty Fresco/*Daily Sketch* 47; Frank Griffin/EMI 135; Hanne Jordan Front Cover, 148, Back Cover; Ken Lambert/EMI 1, 19; Peter Lewry/Nigel Goodall 109, 138; Mayfair Studios 144(TR); *New Musical Express* 22(T), 26, 30(T), 36, 46; PWL 141, 144(TL); Bent K. Rasmussen 65; The Cliff Richard Organisation 105, 176(BR); Roundhouse Studios 123; Sarm Studios 147; Margaret Taylor/Stanfords 125, 172(TR), 174(BR), 175(T), 175(BL), 175(BR), 176(T); Peter Vernon/EMI 142; Unknown 17(T), 17(BL), 34, 52, 58, 72, 115, 116, 127.

All other photographs, studio documentation and other sleeves licenced from EMI Records Ltd.

Introduction

The book consists of twelve main chapters. They all open with general information on the records released and their respective chart placings; the first column representing the A-side and, if applicable, the second column representing the B-side. After this there is a listing and general comments on the recordings made during the years under discussion. The comments concentrate on Cliff's career from an artistic and commercial point of view. There are also notes for collectors, where applicable.

The second part of each chapter lists all the recordings in chronological order, and each session is dealt with under the following four main headings:

1 Identification of the session
   (a) First line specifies for whom the sessions were recorded
   (b) Second line specifies dates for the recording session
   (c) Third line specifies name and location of recording studio/venue

2 List of tracks recorded
   (a) First from left, wherever available, is the master take number
        (sp = splice)
   (b) Song title
   (c) Record on which track first appeared

3 List of participating musicians
   (a) Instrument
   (b) Name of musician

4 Studio personnel and technical details
   (a) Producer
   (b) Engineer(s)
   (c) Additional information on studio
   (d) Session hours

Unfortunately, the information on the sessions is not always complete, and in these instances a dash will be added to the blank spaces.

We cannot accurately determine whether all the unissued tracks listed in this book are complete, incomplete, false starts, out-takes or simply unsuitable for commercial release, as the only unreleased tapes listened to were those recorded at the ABC Theatre, Kingston on 7 March 1962, and these have been fully documented in the respective chapter.

The book contains a complete UK discography of first releases (re-releases on mid-price and budget labels are not listed). A complete index of song titles is included as well, giving cross-references to the session pages where each track is listed. For your convenience, there is also a technical index where terms that are unfamiliar are explained. The book does not deal with bootlegs – illegal recordings, or amateur recordings of live performances.

1

Established 1958

1958–1959

The Records

Schoolboy Crush / Move It	Single	
Move It / Schoolboy Crush	Single	2 / —
High Class Baby /		
My Feet Hit The Ground	Single	7 / —
Livin' Lovin' Doll /		
Steady With You	Single	20 / —
Mean Streak / Never Mind	Single	10 / 21
Living Doll / Apron Strings	Single	1 / —
Travellin' Light / Dynamite	Single	1 / 16
Serious Charge	EP	
Cliff No. 1	EP	
Cliff No. 2	EP	
Oh Boy!	LP	
Cliff	LP	4
Cliff Sings	LP	2

When Cliff's first single hit the shops *Schoolboy Crush* was the intended A-side, but teenagers' reaction to the B-side resulted in the disc being flipped sending *Move It* into the charts to peak at number 2. Though the follow-up singles did not equal the success of *Move It*, they all did extremely well. *High Class Baby*, *Livin' Lovin' Doll* and *Mean Streak* all managed to sail into the top twenty. The next two singles, however, proved to be very strong indeed with both *Living Doll* and *Travellin' Light* reaching the number 1 position. So successful was the latter that even the B-side climbed into the top twenty to reach number 16.

Album sales were impressive as well. The brilliant debut album CLIFF reached the fourth position on the album chart but, surprisingly, the TV soundtrack album OH BOY!, for which Cliff featured on seven tracks, failed to register at all. The picture was definitely better as far as the second album was concerned. CLIFF SINGS was the first one to reach the number 2 slot.

The EPs turned out to be big sellers too, although these were issued before a chart for them had been introduced. SERIOUS CHARGE was hooked up to the release of the film, but in fact were studio recordings, while CLIFF NO. 1 and CLIFF NO. 2 were culled from the debut album.

Collectors' Notes

Apart from the acetate of Cliff's first recording mentioned later, there are a few others. On 7″ and 10″ Emidisc are acetates of *We Had It Made*, although it is unknown whether these are unreleased versions from the May 1959 sessions, or the version as used on the ME AND MY SHADOWS album. Another gem from this period is a 7″ double-sided acetate of two unreleased tracks *Who's Gonna Take You Home* and *Let's Stick Together*. These items were supposedly recorded sometime in 1959, but we cannot track down any further information on them. That's not all for 1959, for Columbia released the rehearsal take of *Apron Strings* on the B-side of *Living Doll* by mistake.

The Sessions

Private recordings: London
Studio sessions for Columbia: Abbey Road
TV soundtrack recordings for ABC TV
Live recordings for Columbia: Abbey Road
Serious Charge soundtrack sessions:
    Abbey Road
Expresso Bongo soundtrack sessions:
    Abbey Road

The first known studio recordings can be traced back to mid-1958, when Cliff Richard and the Drifters – with the line-up of Cliff on guitar and vocals, Terry Smart on drums, and Ian Samwell, Norman Mitham and Ken Pavey on guitars – cut their first demo at the recording studio located on the first floor of the HMV record store near London's Marble Arch. It was here that *Breathless* and *Lawdy Miss Clawdy* were recorded, providing Columbia producer Norrie Paramor with a demonstration tape that resulted with an audition, and Cliff being signed by EMI to their Columbia label on 9 August. Although rumour suggests that acetates were made at the time of these recordings, John Foster, Cliff's first manager, cannot recall having acetate records. He is certain the original tape was used when approaching Norrie Paramor through agent George Ganjou, and considers it possible the tape was retained by one of them, and either they or somebody within the EMI organisation had one or more acetates made, which would explain why there are quite a few around today. There are indications, however, that John had the tape transferred to record for Cliff on 11 September at the same studio where the recordings had been made.

The first Columbia session took place in the EMI studios at Abbey Road on 24 July, strangely enough, 17 days before signing to EMI, although this is regarded as normal procedure as the session was needed to produce both sides that could be released as a single. To minimise any problems of recording with the untried Drifters, session men Ernie Shears on guitar and Frank Clarke on bass were called in to back Cliff, while Terry Smart was the only member of the Drifters to work on the session. It is unknown whether Ian Samwell played or even attended.

The material selected for recording was a cover of a track by American Bobby Helms, *Schoolboy Crush*, as the intended A-side. On the flip was to be a British rock 'n' roll original, written by Ian Samwell, but as was noted earlier in this chapter, the disc was flipped, and *Move It* became the smash hit.

In October, both sides for the follow-up single were taped, *High Class Baby* and *My Feet Hit The Ground*. A third track, *Don't Bug Me Baby*, was also recorded, but has remained unreleased. Unfortunately, we have not been able to track down the names of the musicians on this session, but it seems likely that it was the same line up as in July. The session on 21 October was for soundtrack recordings for ABC-TV's OH BOY! album, with Cliff recording the vocals after the rhythm track sessions. The seven tracks recorded here all appeared on the album.

The November sessions provided some A-sides for singles, and was the first time that the Drifters worked with Cliff in the studio, although by now, the line-up had changed to Jet Harris on bass, Hank Marvin and Bruce Welch on guitars and Terry Smart on drums. For the next sessions in February 1959, Tony Meehan had replaced Terry Smart, and the Mike Sammes Singers helped out on the back-up vocal work. The sessions on the 9th and 10th were live recordings taped before a specially invited audience of 200 fans during two nights at Abbey Road's studio 2, and provided the material for the debut album CLIFF. Of the material, interest was focused on a string of spirited performances of mostly solid rock repertoire, with the Drifters only featured on three of the tracks. Although both *It's Only Make Believe* and *Kisses Sweeter Than Wine* were recorded, they were dropped from the final selection on the album. It is uncertain for what reason, but in all probability it was likely to have been for over-running the duration time of the album. There are, of course, other possibilities such as copyright entanglements or artistic valuations.

The next two sessions turned up some items of interest. In April, Cliff cut the soundtrack sides for his first feature film "Serious Charge" but re-recorded a new country version of *Living Doll* for record release as the version in the film had to bear an authentic rock 'n' roll stamp in keeping with the setting of the movie. From a commercial point of view, the film version was not satisfactory for release as a single or album track. For the next session in May Cliff put down his vocal for *A Teenager In Love* during a Drifters remake session of *Jet Black* and *Driftin'*. This track has not been released on record, probably for the reason that Marty Wilde had a hit with the same song around this time.

The September 1959 sessions provided the material for the CLIFF SINGS album. Some fine orchestral arrangements of standards in the ballad genre were taped with accompaniment by the Norrie Paramor Strings, which would make up fifty per cent of the album content. To be included on the other half of the album were some excellent covers of rock 'n' roll material with the backing by the famous Drifters line-up, who by this time had become the Shadows, due to the UK success of an American vocal group also using the Drifters tag. The album showed that Cliff could do other things than just sing rock 'n' roll and for that reason alone fully deserved the praise Cliff received for it in 1959.

The sessions running through to December produced soundtrack recordings for Cliff's second feature film "Expresso Bongo" as well as a number of A and B-sides.

**Private recordings
Mid-1958
HMV Records, Oxford Street, London**

| — | *Lawdy Miss Clawdy* | *Unissued* |
| — | *Breathless* | *Unissued* |

Guitars: Ian Samwell
        Norman Mitham
        Ken Pavey
Drums: Terry Smart

Engineer: —
Session hours: —

**Studio session for Columbia
24 July 1958
Abbey Road**

| — | Schoolboy Crush | B-side |
| — | Move It | A-side |

Guitars: Ernie Shears
        —

Bass: Frank Clarke
Drums: Terry Smart
Vocals: —

Producer: Norrie Paramor
Engineer: Malcolm Addy
Recorded in studio 2
Session hours: 7.00 pm–10.30 pm

Acetate of Cliff's first private recording 1958.

Studio session for Columbia
3 October 1958
Abbey Road

—	High Class Baby	A-side
—	My Feet Hit The Ground	B-side
—	*Don't Bug Me Baby*	*Unissued*

Guitars: —

—

Stand-up bass: —
Drums: —
Bongos: —
Bass guitar: —

Producer: Norrie Paramor
Engineer: Malcolm Addy
Recorded in studio 2
Session hours: 2.00 pm–5.00 pm

COLUMBIA   C   2869

INSTRUCTIONS FOR RECORDING

Miss SUDBU(3 copies)
ARTIST'S DRTMENT
Mr BARRELI

Date   23rd July, 1958

SIZE	TITLE OF WORK	PUBLISHER	
	SCHOOLBOY CRUSH	Aberbach	DJ lacquers req'd
	MOVE IT	M.S.	DJ lacquers req'd
	To be recorded by CLIFF RICHARD and the Drifters. Thursday 24th July, 1958. Studio No.2 7-10pm	2 non process lacquers of each title for Mr Paramor	
		Curve by arrangement	
	Echo Curve bender Limiter	Engineer MESSRS. ELTHAM BOWN	
	Combination 2 Girls 7 - 9pm 2 Guitars 3 Boys Bass 5 Drums		
	4		RECEIPT

MR. NORRIE PARAMOR IN ATTENDANCE

Documentation from a historic day.

Moment of greatness. Cliff and session musicians recording at EMI's studio 2 in Abbey Road, North London.

Cover for sheet music of Cliff's first hit.

The original Columbia label. Green with silver lettering.

WITH ACKNOWLEDGMENTS TO THE A.B.C. TELEVISION PRODUCTION

TV soundtrack recordings for ABC-TV
21 October 1958
Abbey Road

—	TV Hop	Oh Boy!
—	King Creole	Oh Boy!
—	High School Confidential	Oh Boy!
—	Rockin' Robin	Oh Boy!
—	Early In The Morning	Oh Boy!
—	Somebody Touched Me	Oh Boy!
—	I'll Try	Oh Boy!

Oh Boy Band

Producer: Norrie Paramor
Engineer: —
Recorded in studio 2
Session hours: 6.00 pm–8.00 pm

Backing tracks were recorded on 19 October.

Studio session for Columbia
14 November 1958
Abbey Road

—	Livin' Lovin' Doll	A-side
—	Mean Streak	A-side

Guitars: Hank Marvin
      Bruce Welch
Bass: Jet Harris
Drums: Terry Smart

Producer: Norrie Paramor
Engineers: Peter Bown / Stuart Eltham
Recorded in studio 2
Session hours: 6.00 pm–9.00 pm

Studio session for Columbia
19 November 1958
Abbey Road

—	*Never Mind*	*Unissued*
—	Steady With You	B-side

Guitars: Hank Marvin
      Bruce Welch
Bass: Jet Harris
Drums: Terry Smart
Vocals: Mike Sammes Singers

Producer: Norrie Paramor
Engineers: Peter Bown / Stuart Eltham
Recorded in studio 2
Session hours: 2.00 pm–5.30 pm

Studio session for Columbia
9 February 1959
Abbey Road

—	*It's Only Make Believe*	*Unissued*
—	Apron Strings	Cliff
—	My Babe	Cliff
—	Down The Line	Cliff
—	I Got A Feeling	Cliff
—	Jet Black	Cliff
—	Baby I Don't Care	Cliff
—	Donna	Cliff
—	Move It	Cliff

Guitars: Hank Marvin
      Bruce Welch
Bass: Jet Harris
Drums: Tony Meehan
Vocals: Mike Sammes Singers

Producer: Norrie Paramor
Engineers: Peter Bown / Stuart Eltham
Recorded in studio 2
Session hours: 7.00 pm–10.00 pm

Recorded before a specially invited audience.
Jet Black performed by the Drifters.

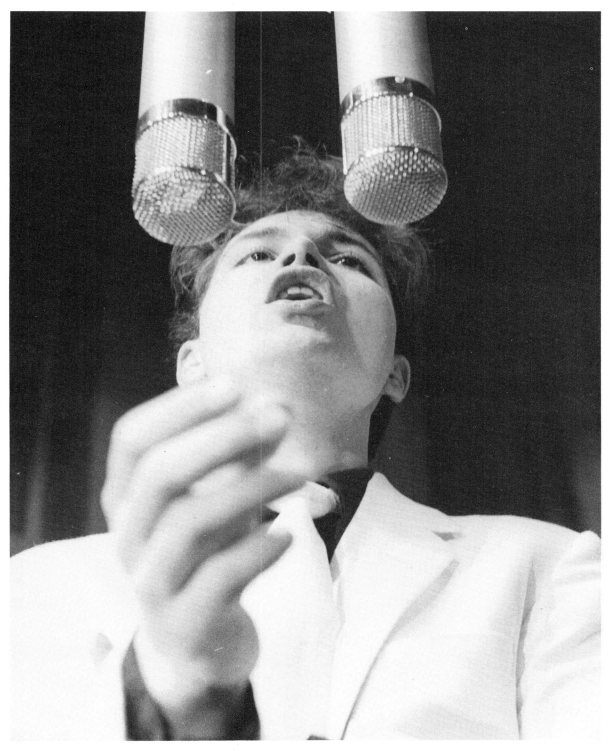

Cliff during the recording of the debut album at EMI's studio 2 in Abbey Road. 9 February 1959.

Studio session for Columbia
10 February 1959
Abbey Road

—	Ready Teddy	Cliff
—	Too Much	Cliff
—	Don't Bug Me Baby	Cliff
—	Driftin'	Cliff
—	That'll Be The Day	Cliff
—	Be Bop A Lula	Cliff
—	Danny	Cliff
—	Whole Lotta Shakin' Goin' On	Cliff
—	*Kisses Sweeter Than Wine*	*Unissued*

Guitars: Hank Marvin
　　　　Bruce Welch
Bass: Jet Harris
Drums: Tony Meehan
Vocals: Mike Sammes Singers

Producer: Norrie Paramor
Engineers: Peter Bown / Stuart Eltham
Recorded in studio 2
Session hours: 7.00 pm–10.00 pm

Recorded before a specially invited audience.

Driftin' / Be Bop A Lula performed by the Drifters.

A typical Cliff Emitape box with content detail.

**Studio session for Columbia
9 March 1959
Abbey Road**

—	Never Mind	B-side
—	*Choppin' 'n' Changin'*	*Unissued*
05	*Dynamite*	*Unissued*

Guitars: Hank Marvin
         Bruce Welch
Bass: Jet Harris
Drums: Tony Meehan

Producer: Norrie Paramor
Engineers: Peter Bown / Stuart Eltham
Recorded in studio 2
Session hours: 7.00 pm–midnight

**Film soundtrack recordings for Serious
Charge
28 April 1959
Abbey Road**

—	Living Doll	A-side
—	No Turning Back	Serious Charge EP
—	Mad About You	Serious Charge EP

Guitars: Hank Marvin
         Bruce Welch

Bass: Jet Harris
Drums: Tony Meehan

Producer: Norrie Paramor
Engineers: Peter Bown / Stuart Eltham
Recorded in studio 2
Session hours: 2.30 pm–5.30 pm

**Studio session for Columbia
4 May 1959
Abbey Road**

—	*A Teenager In Love*	*Unissued*

Guitars: Hank Marvin
         Bruce Welch
Bass: Jet Harris
Drums: Tony Meehan

Producer: Norrie Paramor
Engineers: Peter Bown / Stuart Eltham
Recorded in studio 2
Session hours: 6.00 pm–9.00 pm

**Studio session for Columbia
25 May 1959
Abbey Road**

—	Apron Strings	B-side
—	*We Had It Made*	*Unissued*

Guitars: Hank Marvin
         Bruce Welch
Bass: Jet Harris
Drums: Tony Meehan

Producer: Norrie Paramor
Engineers: Peter Bown / Stuart Eltham
Recorded in studio 2
Session hours: 6.30 pm–10.00 pm

**Studio session for Columbia
25 July 1959
Abbey Road**

34	*Choppin' 'n' Changin'*	*Unissued*
51	*Dynamite*	*Unissued*
15	Travellin' Light	A-side

Typical EMI promotional ad in 'New Musical Express'.
2 October 1959.

Guitars: Hank Marvin
        Bruce Welch
Bass: Jet Harris
Drums: Tony Meehan

Producer: Norrie Paramor
Engineers: Peter Bown/Stuart Eltham
Recorded in studio 2
Session hours: 6.00 pm–10.00 pm

Studio session for Columbia
26 July 1959
Abbey Road

13	*I Gotta Know*	*Unissued*
11	*The Snake And The*	
	Bookworm	*Unissued*
13	*I'm Willing To Learn*	*Unissued*
63	*We Have It Made*	*Unissued*

Guitars: Hank Marvin
        Bruce Welch
Bass: Jet Harris
Drums: Tony Meehan

A typical recording session sheet from Abbey Road.

At EMI's studio 2 in Abbey Road cutting the CLIFF SINGS album with the Norrie Paramor Orchestra.

Producer: Norrie Paramor
Engineers: Peter Bown / Stuart Eltham
Recorded in studio 2
Session hours: 6.00 pm–10.00 pm

Studio session for Columbia
6 September 1959
Abbey Road

—	*Choppin' 'n' Changin'*	*Unissued*
—	Dynamite	A-side
—	I Gotta Know	Cliff Sings
—	The Snake And The Bookworm	Cliff Sings
06	Here Comes Summer	Cliff Sings
—	Twenty Flight Rock	Cliff Sings

Guitars: Hank Marvin
       Bruce Welch
Bass: Jet Harris
Drums: Tony Meehan

Producer: Norrie Paramor
Engineers: Peter Bown / Norman Smith
Recorded in studio 2
Session hours: 6.00 pm–9.50 pm

Studio session for Columbia
7 September 1959
Abbey Road

07	Blue Suede Shoes	Cliff Sings
03	Mean Woman Blues	Cliff Sings
12	Pointed Toe Shoes	Cliff Sings

Guitars: Hank Marvin
       Bruce Welch
Bass: Jet Harris
Drums: Tony Meehan

Producer: Norrie Paramor
Engineers: Peter Bown / Stuart Eltham
Recorded in studio 2
Session hours: 7.00 pm–10.00 pm

Studio session for Columbia
8 September 1959
Abbey Road

05	I'm Walkin'	Cliff Sings
05	Love	Expresso Bongo EP

Guitars: Hank Marvin
        Bruce Welch
Bass: Jet Harris
Drums: Tony Meehan

Producer: Norrie Paramor
Engineers: Peter Bown / Stuart Eltham
Recorded in studio 2
Session hours: 7.00 pm–10.00 pm

**Studio session for Columbia
9 September 1959
Abbey Road**

05	That's My Desire	Cliff Sings
06	Little Things Mean A Lot	Cliff Sings
01	I'll String Along With You	Cliff Sings
10	Somewhere Along The Way	Cliff Sings

The Norrie Paramor Orchestra

Producer: Norrie Paramor
Engineers: Malcolm Addy / Alan Kane
Recorded in studio 2
Session hours: 7.00 pm–10.00 pm

**Studio session for Columbia
10 September 1959
Abbey Road**

14	Embraceable You	Cliff Sings
03	I Don't Know Why	Cliff Sings
14	As Time Goes By	Cliff Sings
04	The Touch Of Your Lips	Cliff Sings

The Norrie Paramor Orchestra

Producer: Norrie Paramor
Engineers: Peter Bown / Stuart Eltham
Recorded in studio 1
Session hours: 7.00 pm–10.15 pm

**Studio session for Columbia
19 October 1959
Abbey Road**

| 06 | The Shrine On The Second Floor | Expresso Bongo EP |

| — | *Fall In Love With You* | *Unissued* |

Guitars: Hank Marvin
        Bruce Welch
Bass: Jet Harris
Drums: Tony Meehan

Producer: Norrie Paramor
Engineers: Malcolm Addy / Peter Bown
Recorded in studio 2
Session hours: 2.30 pm–5.30 pm

**Studio session for Columbia
6 November 1959
Abbey Road**

| *12* | *Don't Be Mad At Me* | *Unissued* |
| *12* | *Willie And The Hand Jive* | *Unissued* |

Guitars: Hank Marvin
        Bruce Welch
Bass: Jet Harris
Drums: Tony Meehan

Producer: Norrie Paramor
Engineers: Peter Bown / Stuart Eltham
Recorded in studio 2
Session hours: 2.30 pm–5.30 pm

**Studio session for Columbia
17 November 1959
Abbey Road**

| — | *Fall In Love With You* | *Unissued* |
| — | *Don't Be Mad At Me* | *Unissued* |

Guitars: Hank Marvin
        Bruce Welch
Bass: Jet Harris
Drums: Tony Meehan

Producer: Norrie Paramor
Engineers: Peter Bown / Stuart Eltham
Recorded in studio 2
Session hours: 7.00 pm–10.00 pm

Studio session for Columbia
18 November 1959
Abbey Road

35	Fall In Love With You	A-side
14	Don't Be Mad At Me	B-side
10	Willie And The Hand Jive	B-side

Guitars: Hank Marvin
　　　　Bruce Welch
Bass: Jet Harris
Drums: Tony Meehan

Producer: Norrie Paramor
Engineers: Peter Bown / Stuart Eltham
Recorded in studio 2
Session hours: 7.00 pm–10.00 pm

Studio session for Columbia
20 December 1959
Abbey Road

—	A Voice In The Wilderness	A-side
—	*Gee But It's Lonesome*	*Unissued*

Guitars: Hank Marvin
　　　　Bruce Welch
Bass: Jet Harris
Drums: Tony Meehan

Producer: Norrie Paramor
Engineer: Malcolm Addy
Recorded in studio 2
Session hours: 11.15 pm–1.00 am

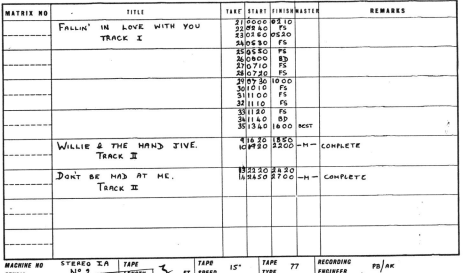

Early promotional ad.
13 October 1961.

For Cliff Richard— they're the tops for the pops

FIDELITY
HF.12 RECORD PLAYER

Weighing only 7 lbs, this remarkably low-priced amplified portable 4-speed record player plays 7″, 10″ or 12″ records. Turnover crystal cartridge gives faithful reproduction. Attractive fibre case in either red/ivory or blue/ivory folkweave. The top of the pops in record player value! (INC P.T.) (200/250 volts, A.C.) **10½ gns**

FIDELITY
ARGYLL MINOR

This all-British tape recorder gives unsurpassed value—twin-track recording at 3½ i.p.s., adjustable tone and volume controls, magic-eye indicator, socket for extension speaker, sockets for recording from radio, gram or microphone. In either red/white or brown/white. Weight 16 lbs. Complete with microphone and tape. (200/250 volts, A.C.) **22 gns**

FIDELITY for sound value

FIDELITY RADIO LIMITED · LONDON · W11

2

The Young Ones

1960–1961

The Records

A Voice In The Wilderness/		
Don't Be Mad At Me	Single	2/—
Fall In Love With You/		
Willie And The Hand Jive	Single	2/—
Please Don't Tease/		
Where Is My Heart	Single	1/—
Nine Times Out Of Ten/		
Thinking Of Our Love	Single	3/—
I Love You/'D' In Love	Single	1/—
Theme For A Dream/		
Mumblin' Mosie	Single	3/—
Gee Whiz It's You/		
I Cannot Find A True Love	Single	4/—
A Girl Like You/		
Now's The Time To Fall In		
Love	Single	3/—
When The Girl In Your Arms/		
Got A Funny Feeling	Single	3/—

Expresso Bongo	EP	(1)*
Cliff Sings No. 1	EP	4
Cliff Sings No. 2	EP	3
Cliff Sings No. 3	EP	2
Cliff Sings No. 4	EP	
Cliff's Silver Discs	EP	1
Me And My Shadows No. 1	EP	5
Me And My Shadows No. 2	EP	8
Me And My Shadows No. 3	EP	6
Listen To Cliff No. 1	EP	17
Dream	EP	3
Listen To Cliff No. 2	EP	

EP chart positions taken from 'Record Retailer'

Me And My Shadows	LP	2
Listen to Cliff	LP	2
21 Today	LP	1
The Young Ones	LP	1

Compared with the impact Cliff made on the charts in 1958 and 1959, the following two years proved to be exceptional. Not only did all nine singles hit the top four, but two of them reached the top spot. *Please Don't Tease* became the first ever single to return to number 1 after dropping from the summit, and *Gee Whiz It's You* became the first ever European single to chart in Britain, although the disc was never officially released in that country.

Album sales were as exceptional as the singles. Two of the four albums reached number 2, while 21 TODAY and THE YOUNG ONES provided the first two consecutive number 1s on the album chart.

DREAM
Cliff Richard
Dream; All I do is dream of you; I'll see you in my dreams; When I grow too old to dream
COLUMBIA SEG8119

A SMOOTH ballad set from Cliff Richard — the sort of set that has widened his circle of appreciation. His voice has a magnetic charm and is full of

warm appeal. These songs — based on a dream theme — will certainly find its place regularly on the turntable.

Well performed, it places him further up that ladder of real professionalism.

The EPs all did well too. Ten of the twelve that were released featured material previously available, and the only conclusion can be the value for money aspect. CLIFF SINGS, ME AND MY SHADOWS and LISTEN TO CLIFF were all culled from the respective albums, while

CLIFF'S SILVER DISCS grouped together four recent singles. The most successful EP of this period was the one containing the soundtrack recordings from "Expresso Bongo"* which became the first to climb into the singles chart.

Collectors' Notes

Two versions were done of the title song for "The Young Ones". The film version featured a different vocal, and as of now is unreleased as it was never intended for record release.

Of the singles pressed in the UK for distribution overseas, we have already discussed *Gee Whiz It's You*, but there was one more during this period that found its way briefly into

UK record outlets. *What'd I Say / Blue Moon* (Columbia DC 758) were two tracks taken from the LISTEN TO CLIFF album and EP.

Spoken items of interest included Christmas messages for EMI, and a personal message specially recorded for release as a flexi-disc given away with 'Serenade' magazine.

The Sessions

Studio sessions for Columbia: Abbey Road
The Young Ones soundtrack sessions:
  Abbey Road

The March 1960 recording sessions were the first of that year and as usual were held at EMI's Abbey Road studio 2. Work was geared towards producing some hit singles, B-sides and album tracks. *Nine Times Out Of Ten*, *Please Don't Tease* and *Gee Whiz It's You* were the gems from these sessions that pioneered the sound Cliff would keep to for the next few years. Usually the sessions started around 7 pm and lasted three hours, allowing three or four tracks to be laid down. Throughout the early sixties this became the basic procedure for recording, with Cliff working the same way, simply and fast, putting down in one session complete takes that could later be chosen as the released master, and keeping overdubbing to a minimum. In fact the only additional recording work on these sessions was done on the 17th when Hank Marvin carried out some guitar solo overdubs on *I Love You So* taking up to an hour of studio time, presumably after the actual session had finished. Most of the recordings during this period featured the usual Shadows line-up – Hank Marvin, Bruce Welch, Jet Harris and Tony Meehan. On the last two 1961 sessions, however, Brian Bennett was brought in as a replacement

CLIFF'S SILVER DISCS
Cliff Richard and The Shadows
Please don't tease; Fall in love with you; Nine times out of ten; Travellin' light.
COLUMBIA SEG8050
ANOTHER winning set from the irresistible Cliff Richard, and each one has been a top seller for this successful young star.

No need for encouragement from me here. You know the high standard to expect from Cliff, and you also know just how exciting these particular tracks are.

Typical reviews from the 'Record Mail'.

LISTEN TO CLIFF
Cliff Richard
What'd I say; Blue Moon; True love will come to you; Lover; Unchained melody; Idle gossip; First lesson in love; Almost like being in love; Beat out dat rhythm on a drum; Memories linger on; Temptation; I live for you; Sentimental journey; I want you to know; We kiss in a shadow; It's you
COLUMBIA 33SX1320
BRITAIN'S very own hit maker Cliff Richard now comes up on Columbia with his fourth LP — and what an exciting recording this is.

With the accompaniments shared by The Shadows, a string orchestra and a swinging band, this polished young entertainer is in tremendous form with a wonderful assortment of numbers.

Give "Blue Moon" and "Lover" a spin, and you'll want to hear more. A top disc which is a must for all Cliff fans and cannot fail to be a big seller.

N. PARAMOR / COLUMBIA

TAPE NO E 38309Z IDENTITY CLIFF RICHARD & THE SHADOWS.

MATRIX NO	TITLE	TAKE	START	FINISH	MASTER	REMARKS
	NINE TIMES OUT OF TEN.	1	0000	0210	2-06	
		2	0230	0440	2-07	
		3	0510	0720	2-07	
		4	0750	FS		
		5	0800	FS		Technically faulty
		6	0820	1030	2-07	
		7	1050	1300	2-03	
		8	1330	FS		
		9	1340	1550	2-04	harmony guitar
		10	1620	BD		vocal distortion PB
		11	1750	2000	2-03	
	I DON'T KNOW.	1	2020	FS		
		2	2040	FS		
		3	2050	2300	2-12	
		4	2330	FS		
		5	2410	BD		
		6	2550	2810	2-12	
						this hasn't been remade to this date 28-9-60

MACHINE NO STEREO 1A No 2 STUDIO _____ TAPE LENGTH 4 FT. TAPE SPEED 15" TAPE TYPE 77 RECORDING ENGINEER PB-AK

DATE 15/2/60 195

DISTRIBUTING ORGANISATION — SALES & SERVICE LTD. HAYES, MIDDLESEX, ENGLAND

for Tony Meehan. Another change in the musician line-up was seen on the sessions that provided the material for the LISTEN TO CLIFF album, when the accompaniments were shared between the Shadows and the Norrie Paramor Orchestra, each representing the rhythm and ballad content of the album, originally to be called STRINGY AND SWINGY.

The first foreign recordings were done towards the end of 1960, when Cliff taped German versions of *Fall In Love With You* and *A Voice In The Wilderness* for future release in that country, a thing he would do from time to time over the next fifteen years.

Cliff went back into the studios again early in 1961, and the sessions on 4 March can be seen as remake sessions. Cliff re-recorded three songs that had first been attempted the previous October, and were needed to fill out the LISTEN TO CLIFF album.

The first session for the "The Young Ones"

soundtrack was set for May, and followed the basic procedure laid down by this time. The studio was again number 2 at Abbey Road, with the Shadows in the familiar line-up, and the Stanley Black Orchestra adding strings on many of the songs to good effect, in order to create the right feel needed for the movie. The next sessions were designed to try some different material, and provided a number of master takes for the 21 TODAY album. Soundtrack sessions resumed in July and ran through into August. Grazina Frame recorded her vocal for overdubbing on to Carole Gray's duet with Cliff on *Nothing Is Impossible* at this time. The vocal taped at the August session is the one featured in the movie and on the soundtrack album.

Almost all of the recording work for the remainder of the year supplied Columbia with some of the material that would later surface on Cliff's only studio album of 1962.

**Studio session for Columbia
15 March 1960
Abbey Road**

11	Nine Times Out Of Ten	A-side
16	I Don't Know	Me And
		My Shadows
05	Thinking Of Our Love	B-side

Guitars: Hank Marvin
          Bruce Welch
Bass: Jet Harris
Drums: Tony Meehan

Producer: Norrie Paramor
Engineers: Peter Bown / Malcolm Addy
Recorded in studio 2
Session hours: 7.00 pm–10.00 pm

EMITAPE

N. Paramor / Columbia

TAPE NO *E 38310 Z* IDENTITY CLIFF RICHARD & THE SHADOWS

MATRIX NO	TITLE	TAKE	START	FINISH	MASTER	REMARKS
	I DON'T KNOW.	7	0000	FS		
		8	0030	FS		
		9	0040	BD		
		10	0240	0450	2·11	
		11	0500	FS		
		12	0510	0720	2·12	
		13	0740	FS		
		14	0800	BD		
		15	0840	FS		
		16	0850	1100		
		17	1120	BD		
		18	1240	1450	2·09	
	THINKING OF OUR LOVE.	1	1500	1740	2·37	
		2	1750	2030	2·33	
		3	2040	2320	2·34	
		4	2340	FS		
		5	2440	2720	–M–	2·36

MACHINE NO STEREO IA
STUDIO No 2   TAPE LENGTH 4   FT. TAPE SPEED 15"   TAPE TYPE 77   RECORDING ENGINEER PB - AK

DATE 15/3/60 195 /

Studio session for Columbia
16 March 1960
Abbey Road

05	Evergreen Tree	Me And My Shadows
15	You're Just The One To Do It	Me And My Shadows
05	Left Out Again	Me And My Shadows

Guitars: Hank Marvin
       Bruce Welch
Bass: Jet Harris
Drums: Tony Meehan
Harmonica: —

Producer: Norrie Paramor
Engineers: Peter Bown / Malcolm Addy
Recorded in studio 2
Session hours: 7.00 pm – 10.00 pm

Studio session for Columbia
17 March 1960
Abbey Road

10	Gee Whiz It's You	A-side
16	I Love You So	Me And My Shadows
07	She's Gone	Me And My Shadows
—	*Speech By Cliff*	*Unissued*

Guitars: Hank Marvin
       Bruce Welch
Bass: Jet Harris
Drums: Tony Meehan

Producer: Norrie Paramor
Engineers: Peter Bown / Malcolm Addy
Recorded in studio 2
Session hours: 7.00 pm – 10.00 pm

Recording sheet from EMI's official files at Abbey Road.

Typical front pages from 'Record Mail', a monthly review of new record releases, distributed and issued by EMI to retailers.

RECORD MAIL

A MONTHLY REVIEW AND DETAILS OF THE LATEST
'POPULAR' RECORDS ISSUED BY E.M.I RECORDS LTD.
H.M.V, Capitol, Columbia, Parlophone,
M-G-M, Mercury, Top Rank.

Vol. 4. No. 5.   May, 1961

'GEE WHIZ!' SAYS CLIFF

1D.

RECORD MAIL REPORTER

ANOTHER success for Columbia singing star Cliff Richard — but this time it's a success with a difference. It concerns his recording of a song called "Gee whiz it's you" — and it might well be put under the heading of The Mystery of the Unsung Hit. 'Unsung' meaning unheralded, of course.

For — unannounced, unpublicised, unexpectedly (and unheralded) — "Gee whiz it's you" raced into the British Hit Parade. 'Unexpected' because it had never been released officially as a 'single' in this country. Taken from Cliff's "Me And My Shadows" LP, it was, in fact, issued several months ago for the overseas market only.

SPECIAL REQUEST

Said a spokesman of E.M.I Records: "We issued this disc of 'Gee whiz' last December at the special request of our overseas distributors. We couldn't release it on the home market at the same time because we had only just issued his 'I love you' single.

"Then came his 'Theme for a dream' — and, as far as we were concerned, 'Gee whiz' was still only a special overseas issue. But somehow — and we don't know how — word of it got back to his British fans. They then asked their dealers for it and the next thing we knew was that it was in the Hit Parade."

ANOTHER SILVER DISC

News of this latest success comes to Cliff at the same time as the announcement that he has won his eighth Silver Disc (awarded by 'Disc') to mark the quarter-million-plus sales of "Theme for a dream." "Gee whiz it's you" is on Columbia 45-DC756.

RECORD MAIL

A MONTHLY REVIEW AND DETAILS OF THE LATEST
'POPULAR' RECORDS ISSUED BY E.M.I RECORDS LTD.
H.M.V, Capitol, Columbia, Parlophone,
M-G-M, Mercury.

Vol. 3.   No. 6.   June, 1960

UNDER-21s ARE GIVEN THE VOTE!

1D.

A Beat Ballot to decide Cliff Richard's new record

AT LAST — the under-21s have been given the vote! But this ballot — held recently in the Conference Room of E.M.I Records' new London headquarters in Manchester Square — was a ballot with a difference. Call it, if you like, a Beat Ballot.

The occasion was a unique one in the history of the recording industry — for these under-21s were given the opportunity of helping to decide which should be Cliff Richard's new disc release. And they made their choice from 21 sides he had already recorded.

The Beat Ballot happened this way. Cliff had his songs "in the can" — but neither he nor recording manager Norrie Paramor could make up their minds which sides to issue next. So the teenage voters were called in.

LISTENING SESSION

As Norrie Paramor himself put it: "We thought it was about time that the fans themselves had a say in deciding Cliff's new release and that it would be a good idea to arrange a listening session at which all 21 sides were played."

This, then, was done. From a dozen youth clubs in and around London came 24 boys and girls — one boy and one girl from each of the clubs. Then there were two dozen members of Cliff's own fan club plus several of the younger members of E.M.I Records' own staff.

INTRODUCTIONS

The session began at 6.15 p.m. and, after introductions had been made, each member of the teenage panel was handed a voting slip. The discs were played — it took just one hour and a quarter to play them all — and the votes were cast.

Then the ballot papers were collected and personnel from the statistical department of E.M.I Records began immediately to work out the results. While all this activity was going on a "Coke and Doughnut Bar" was opened — with great success!

BIG SURPRISE

Big surprise of the evening was the arrival of Cliff Richard himself. The teenagers were waiting to hear which sides had been voted into top places — when in walked Cliff to make the announcement.

And the result of the Beat Ballot? A number called "Please don't tease" written by Cliff's rhythm guitarist, Bruce Welch. Runner-up was "Gee wiz its you". Look out for them — they were the teenagers' choice.

A BIG 'HELLO' from Cliff to all his fans. This is one of many exciting new pictures of the Columbia recording star to be found in this edition of Record Mail.

EXCLUSIVE! PHOTO-FEATURE SPOTLIGHTS CLIFF ON TOUR page 9

Studio session for Columbia
25 March 1960
Abbey Road

—	Please Don't Tease	A-side
—	*Tell Me*	*Unissued*

Guitars: Hank Marvin
       Bruce Welch
Bass: Jet Harris
Drums: Tony Meehan

Producer: Norrie Paramor
Engineer: Malcolm Addy
Recorded in studio 2
Session hours: 7.00 pm–10.00 pm

Studio session for Columbia
30 March 1960
Abbey Road

11	Tell Me	Me And My Shadows
07	Where Is My Heart	B-side
05	Lamp Of Love	Me And My Shadows
10	I'm Gonna Get You	Me And My Shadows
04	I Cannot Find A True Love	Me And My Shadows

Guitars: Hank Marvin
       Bruce Welch
Bass: Jet Harris
Drums: Tony Meehan

Producer: Norrie Paramor
Engineers: Malcolm Addy / Norman Smith
Recorded in studio 2
Session hours: 7.00 pm–10.00 pm

Studio session for Columbia
1 April 1960
Abbey Road

sp	Working After School	Me And My Shadows
07	You And I	Me And My Shadows

11	I Live For You	Listen To Cliff
01	*What'd I Say*	*Unissued*

Guitars: Hank Marvin
       Bruce Welch
Bass: Jet Harris
Drums: Tony Meehan

Producers: Norrie Paramor / J. Schroeder
Engineer: Peter Bown
Recorded in studio 2
Session hours: 7.00 pm–10.00 pm

Working After School is an edit of takes 9 and 11

Studio session for Columbia
24 June 1960
Abbey Road

07	I'm Willing To Learn	Me And My Shadows
06	We Have It Made	Me And My Shadows
07	Choppin' 'n' Changin'	Me And My Shadows
—	*Interview with Dave Sampson*	*Unissued*

Guitars: Hank Marvin
       Bruce Welch
Bass: Jet Harris
Drums: Tony Meehan

Producer: Norrie Paramor
Engineers: Malcolm Addy / Norman Smith
Recorded in studio 2
Session hours: 2.30 pm–5.15 pm

Studio session for Columbia
28 July 1960
Abbey Road

10	Memories Linger On	Listen to Cliff
05	It's You	Listen to Cliff
09	*Now's The Time To Fall In Love*	*Unissued*

Publicity shot from the early sixties. Exact date unknown.

Guitars: Hank Marvin
        Bruce Welch
Bass: Jet Harris
Drums: Tony Meehan

Producer: Norrie Paramor
Engineers: Malcolm Addy / Norman Smith
Recorded in studio 2
Session hours: 2.00 pm–5.00 pm

Studio session for Columbia
9 September 1960
Abbey Road

03	'D' In Love		B-side
10	Catch Me		21 Today
14	I Love You		A-side

Guitars: Hank Marvin
        Bruce Welch
Bass: Jet Harris
Drums: Tony Meehan

Producer: Norrie Paramor
Engineers: Malcolm Addy / David Lloyd
Recorded in studio 2
Session hours: 2.00 pm–5.00 pm

Studio session for Columbia
20 September 1960
Abbey Road

03	*Michelle*		*Unissued*
sp	Now's The Time To Fall In		
	Love		B-side

Guitars: Hank Marvin
        Bruce Welch
Bass: Jet Harris
Drums: Tony Meehan

Producer: Norrie Paramor
Engineer: Malcolm Addy
Recorded in studio 2
Session hours: 2.00 pm–5.00 pm

Now's The Time To Fall In Love is an edit of takes 41 and 42.

Studio session for Columbia
27 September 1960
Abbey Road

—	*Until The Right One Comes Along*	*Unissued*
32	*First Lesson In Love*	*Unissued*
06	*True Love Will Come To You*	*Unissued*

Guitars: Hank Marvin
        Bruce Welch
Bass: Jet Harris
Drums: Tony Meehan

Producer: Norrie Paramor
Engineer: Malcolm Addy
Recorded in studio 2
Session hours: 2.00 pm–5.00 pm

Studio session for Columbia
13 October 1960
Abbey Road

06	True Love Will Come To You	Listen to Cliff
05	*What'd I Say*	*Unissued*
06	First Lesson In Love	Listen to Cliff
01	*Unchained Melody*	*Unissued*
03	*I Want You To Know*	*Unissued*
—	Christmas message for EMI International	
—	Christmas message for EMI South Africa	

Guitars: Hank Marvin
        Bruce Welch
Bass: Jet Harris
Drums: Tony Meehan

Producer: Norrie Paramor
Engineer: Malcolm Addy
Recorded in studio 2
Session hours: 2.00 pm–5.00 pm

True Love Will Come To You / What'd I Say / First Lesson In Love are listed as remakes on the EMI session sheets.

Studio session for Columbia
17 November 1960
Abbey Road

07	We Kiss In The Shadow	Listen to Cliff
05	Idle Gossip	Listen to Cliff
03	Blue Moon	Listen to Cliff
02	Temptation	Listen to Cliff

The Norrie Paramor Orchestra
Drums: Tony Meehan

Producer: Norrie Paramor
Engineers: Malcolm Addy / Norman Smith
Recorded in studio 2
Session hours: 1.30 pm–5.00 pm

Studio session for Columbia
5 December 1960
Abbey Road

—	Bin Verliebt (Fall in Love With You)	German release
—	Die Stimme Der Liebe (Voice In The Wilderness)	German release

Guitars: Hank Marvin
        Bruce Welch
Bass: Jet Harris
Drums: Tony Meehan

Producer: Norrie Paramor
Engineer: Malcolm Addy
Recorded in studio 2
Session hours: 7.00 pm–10.00 pm

Studio session for Columbia
11 January 1961
Abbey Road

03	Almost Like Being In Love	Listen to Cliff
08	Lover	Listen to Cliff
—	Beat Out Dat Rhythm On A Drum	Listen to Cliff
06	Sentimental Journey	Listen to Cliff

The Bernard Ebbinghouse Orchestra

Producer: Norrie Paramor
Engineers: Malcolm Addy / David Lloyd
Recorded in studio 2
Session hours: 7.00 pm–10.00 pm

Studio session for Columbia
28 January 1961
Abbey Road

—	Theme For A Dream	A-side
04	Tough Enough	21 Today
08	*Poor Boy*	*Unissued*
—	Mumblin' Mosie	B-side
—	A Girl Like You	A-side

Guitars: Hank Marvin
              Bruce Welch
Bass: Jet Harris
Drums: Tony Meehan
Bongos: Tommy Kamara
Vocals: Mike Sammes Singers

Producer: Norrie Paramor
Engineer: Malcolm Addy
Recorded in studio 2
Session hours: 2.00 pm–5.00 pm and
7.00 pm–10.00 pm

Studio session for Columbia
30 January 1961
Abbey Road

03	How Wonderful To Know	21 Today
05	A Mighty Lonely Man	21 Today
06	To Prove My Love For You	21 Today
04	Outsider	21 Today
04	Fifty Tears For Every Kiss	21 Today
—	When The Girl In Your Arms	A-side

The Norrie Paramor Orchestra
Vocals: Mike Sammes Singers

Producer: Norrie Paramor
Engineer: Malcolm Addy
Recorded in studio 2
Session hours: 3.00 pm–6.00 pm and
7.00 pm–10.00 pm

Studio session for Columbia
4 March 1961
Abbey Road

38	I Want You To Know	Listen to Cliff

31	Unchained Melody	Listen to Cliff
33	What'd I Say	Listen to Cliff
01	*My Blue Heaven*	*Unissued*

Guitars: Hank Marvin
            Bruce Welch
Bass: Jet Harris
Drums: Tony Meehan

Producer: Norrie Paramor
Engineers: Malcolm Addy / David Lloyd
Recorded in studio 2
Session hours: midday–3.00 pm

I Want You To Know / Unchained Melody / What'd I Say are all listed as remakes on the EMI session sheets..

**Studio session for Columbia
10 April 1961
Abbey Road**

—	Schön Wie Ein Traum (Theme For A Dream)	German release
—	Vreneli	German release

Guitars: Hank Marvin
            Bruce Welch
Bass: Jet Harris
Drums: Tony Meehan

Producer: Norrie Paramor
Engineer: Malcolm Addy
Recorded in studio 2
Session hours: 7.00 pm–9.00 pm

**Studio session for Columbia
19 April 1961
Abbey Road**

12	Poor Boy	21 Today
06	My Blue Heaven	21 Today
07	Got A Funny Feeling	B-side

Guitars: Hank Marvin
            Bruce Welch
Bass: Jet Harris
Drums: Tony Meehan
Piano: —

Producer: Norrie Paramor
Engineers: Malcolm Addy / Norman Smith
Recorded in studio 1
Session hours: midday–3.15 pm

Poor Boy / My Blue Heaven are listed as remakes on the EMI session sheets.

**Studio session for Columbia
4 May 1961
Abbey Road**

06	Dream	Dream EP
13	All I Do Is Dream Of You	Dream EP
13	I'll See You In My Dreams	Dream EP

Guitars: Hank Marvin
            Bruce Welch
Bass: Jet Harris
Drums: Tony Meehan

Producer: Norrie Paramor
Engineer: Malcolm Addy
Recorded in studio 2
Session hours: 7.00 pm–10.00 pm

**Studio session for Columbia
12 May 1961
Abbey Road**

08	When I Grow Too Old To Dream	Dream EP

Guitars: Hank Marvin
            Bruce Welch
Bass: Jet Harris
Drums: Tony Meehan

Producer: Norrie Paramor
Engineer: Malcolm Addy
Recorded in studio 2
Session hours: 7.00 pm–10.00 pm

Film soundtrack recordings for
The Young Ones
23 May 1961
Abbey Road

36	*The Young Ones*	*Unissued*
07	*When The Girl In Your Arms*	*Unissued*
07	*Gotta Funny Feeling*	*Unissued*

Guitars: Hank Marvin
       Bruce Welch
Bass: Jet Harris
Drums: Tony Meehan

Producer: Norrie Paramor
Engineers: Malcolm Addy / Norman Smith
Recorded in studio 2
Session hours: 7.00 pm–10.15 pm

In the EMI ledgers these three tracks from the film "The Young Ones" are marked as remakes and also there is mention of Associated British Picture Corporation. From this we can assume that they are the versions featured in the film.

Studio session for Columbia
4 July 1961
Abbey Road

08	Tea For Two	21 Today
05	Forty Days	21 Today
05	The Night Is So Lonely	21 Today

Guitars: Hank Marvin
       Bruce Welch
Bass: Jet Harris
Drums: Tony Meehan

Producer: Norrie Paramor
Engineer: Malcolm Addy
Recorded in studio 2
Session hours: 7.00 pm–10.00 pm

Studio session for Columbia
11 July 1961
Abbey Road

04	Without You	21 Today
18	Y'Arriva	21 Today
20	Shame On You	21 Today

Guitars: Hank Marvin
       Bruce Welch
Bass: Jet Harris
Drums: Tony Meehan

Producer: Norrie Paramor
Engineer: Malcolm Addy
Recorded in studio 2
Session hours: 7.00 pm–10.15 pm

Studio session for Columbia
28 July 1961
Abbey Road

21	Happy Birthday	21 Today
06	We Say Yeah	The Young Ones
10	*Lessons In Love*	*Unissued*

Guitars: Hank Marvin
       Bruce Welch
Bass: Jet Harris
Drums: Tony Meehan

Producer: Norrie Paramor
Engineers: Malcolm Addy / Norman Smith
Recorded in studio 2
Session hours: 7.45 pm–10.30 pm

Film soundtrack recordings for
The Young Ones
9 August 1961
Abbey Road

05	Vaudeville Routine (Part 1)	The Young Ones
08	Vaudeville Routine (Part 2)	The Young Ones
13	Vaudeville Routine (Part 3)	The Young Ones
15	Vaudeville Routine (Part 4)	The Young Ones
22	Vaudeville Routine (Part 5)	The Young Ones
02	No One For Me But Nicki	The Young Ones
04	Nothing Is Impossible	The Young Ones

08	Friday Night (See You At The Dance)	The Young Ones
—	All For One	The Young Ones
—	Mambo	The Young Ones

The Stanley Black Orchestra

Producer: Norrie Paramor
Engineers: Malcolm Addy / Alan Kane
Recorded in studio 2
Session hours: 2.30 pm–6.00 pm and 7.00 pm–10.00 pm

Tracks on Vaudeville Routine: What Do You Know We Got A Show / Have A Smile For Everyone You Meet / Tinkle, Tinkle / The Eccentric / Algy The Piccadilly Johnny / Captain Ginjah / Joshua / Where Did You Get That Hat / What Do You Know We Got A Show / Living Doll.

Nothing Is Impossible is a duet with Grazina Frame and No One For Me But Nicki is a Grazina Frame only vocal.

**Film soundtrack recordings for
The Young Ones
11 August 1961
Abbey Road**

36	The Young Ones	The Young Ones
36	Lessons In Love	The Young Ones
11	*What Is There To Say*	*Unissued*

Guitars: Hank Marvin
        Bruce Welch
Bass: Jet Harris
Drums: Tony Meehan

Producers: J. Schroeder / Norrie Paramor
Engineers: Malcolm Addy / David Lloyd
Recorded in studio 2
Session hours: 7.00 pm–10.30 pm

**Studio session for Columbia
4 December 1961
Abbey Road**

| 04 | I Wake Up Cryin' | 32 Minutes And 17 Seconds |

05	Spanish Harlem	32 Minutes And 17 Seconds
08	Let's Make A Memory	32 Minutes And 17 Seconds
—	*Do You Remember*	*Unissued*

The Norrie Paramor Orchestra
The Mike Sammes Singers

Producer: Norrie Paramor
Engineers: Malcolm Addy / Norman Smith
Recorded in studio 2
Session hours: 2.30 pm–5.45 pm

**Studio session for Columbia
5 December 1961
Abbey Road**

—	Secret Love	Love Songs EP
03	How Long Is Forever	32 Minutes And 17 Seconds
—	*The Young Ones*	*Unissued*
06	Falling In Love With Love	32 Minutes And 17 Seconds

The Norrie Paramor Orchestra

Producer: Norrie Paramor
Engineer: Malcolm Addy
Recorded in studio 2
Session hours: 2.30 pm–5.30 pm

**Studio session for Columbia
11 December 1961
Abbey Road**

02	Love Letters	Love Songs EP
02	I'm Looking Out The Window	A-side
08	*In Other Words*	*Unissued*
06	Who Are We To Say	32 Minutes And 17 Seconds

The Norrie Paramor Orchestra

Producer: Norrie Paramor
Engineer: Malcolm Addy
Recorded in studio 2
Session hours: 2.30 pm–5.30 pm

Studio session for Columbia
18 December 1961
Abbey Road

07	You Don't Know	32 Minutes And 17 Seconds
—	*Take Special Care*	*Unissued*
10	So I've Been Told	32 Minutes And 17 Seconds

Guitars: Hank Marvin
        Bruce Welch
Bass: Jet Harris
Drums: Tony Meehan

Producer: Norrie Paramor
Engineer: Malcolm Addy
Recorded in studio 2
Session hours: 2.30 pm–5.30 pm

Studio session for Columbia
19 December 1961
Abbey Road

03	Do You Want To Dance	B-side
12	Since I Lost You	B-side

Guitars: Hank Marvin
        Bruce Welch
Bass: Jet Harris
Drums: Tony Meehan

Producer: Norrie Paramor
Engineer: Malcolm Addy
Recorded in studio 2
Session hours: 2.30 pm–5.30 pm

3

Summer Holiday

1962–1963

The Records

The Young Ones / We Say Yeah	Single	1 / —		Cliff Richard No. 2	EP	19
I'm Looking Out The Window /				Time For Cliff Richard And		
Do You Want To Dance	Single	2 / 10		The Shadows	EP	
It'll Be Me / Since I Lost You	Single	2 / —		Holiday Carnival	EP	1
The Next Time / Bachelor Boy	Single	1 / 1		Hits From Summer Holiday	EP	4
Summer Holiday /				More Hits From Summer		
Dancing Shoes	Single	1 / —		Holiday	EP	
Lucky Lips / I Wonder	Single	4 / —		Cliff's Lucky Lips	EP	17
It's All In The Game /				Love Songs	EP	4
Your Eyes Tell On You	Single	2 / —				
Don't Talk To Him /				EP chart positions taken from 'Record Retailer'		
Say You're Mine	Single	2 / —				
				32 Minutes And 17 Seconds With		
				Cliff Richard	LP	3
Cliff's Hit Parade	EP	4		Summer Holiday	LP	1
Cliff Richard No. 1	EP	4		Cliff's Hit Album	LP	2
Hits From The Young Ones	EP	11		When In Spain	LP	8

CLIFF RICHARD
Forty days; Catch me; How wonderful to know; Tough enough
COLUMBIA SEG8151

CLIFF rings the changes on this one, varying the pace and content expertly.

With The Shadows laying down the beat he rocks powerfully through Chuck Berry's "Forty Days", eases up for the lilting "Catch me", with support from a coy-sounding female chorus. On the other side he has the Norrie Paramor Orchestra in support for a tender ballad, "How wonderful to know" before The Shadows rejoin him for the rousing finale, "Tough enough".

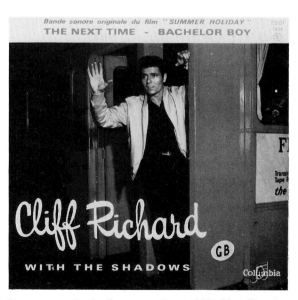

Picture cover for the European release of *The Next Time/ Bachelor Boy.*

Change of style for the Columbia label. Now black with silver lettering.

The years 1962 and 1963 were the most successful for Cliff since the late fifties. Of the eight singles released in this period *The Young Ones* was the first to be released to advance sales of more than one million copies and was to become the biggest seller of all of Cliff's singles so far. It entered the charts at number 1, and stayed on the chart for 21 weeks. The remaining singles did extremely well, all hitting the top four, and two of them reaching the top spot. *I'm Looking Out The Window/Do You Want To Dance* proved to be a very strong release

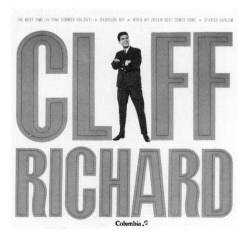

A rare EP sleeve from Europe.

indeed with both sides fighting each other all the way up the charts, thus probably preventing either of them reaching the top spot. Eventually they made it to an impressive 2nd and 10th placing. *The Next Time/Bachelor Boy* did even better with both sides reaching the number 1 spot, and *Summer Holiday* repeated the success of *Please Don't Tease* by returning to number 1 after dropping from the summit.

Album sales were just as impressive. The SUMMER HOLIDAY soundtrack enjoyed a spell at the pinnacle of the charts, but ironically the only regular studio album of 1962 – 32 MINUTES AND 17 SECONDS – reached the third position only, whereas the compilation CLIFF'S HIT ALBUM reached the number 2 spot, largely as a result of the sound idea of collecting fourteen of Cliff's singles on one album. Another sign of Cliff's broadening popularity was the eighth position reached on the British album chart by the foreign language recording WHEN IN SPAIN, despite the fact that most British fans could not understand the lyrics!

Although none of the EPs showed up on the singles bestseller charts during this period, all proved to be consistent sellers. The only two to feature new material were HOLIDAY CARNIVAL and LOVE SONGS, while the others recycled tracks from recent singles and albums.

Collectors' Notes

Some mystery surrounds the song *Bachelor Boy* from the SUMMER HOLIDAY soundtrack, where the version that was originally recorded for the film is slightly different from the version that was eventually released. According to one tape box, there is also a special version for the USA, although it seems likely that this is a remix of the record version.

The Sessions

Studio sessions for Columbia: Abbey Road
Live Recordings for Columbia: ABC Kingston
Summer Holiday soundtrack sessions:
 Abbey Road
Studio sessions for Columbia: EMI Barcelona
Studio sessions for Columbia: Blackpool

Cliff visited EMI's Abbey Road Studios to do some regular recording work in January, and laid down two more tracks for 32 MINUTES AND 17 SECONDS, although another session was set for May to complete the album. In the meantime and to collect sufficient material for a

TAPE No. E 463 99 Z   IDENTITY "THE CLIFF RICHARD SHOW"   STEREO
"SECOND HOUSE"

MATRIX No.	TITLE	TAKE	START	FINISH	MASTER	REMARKS
	"LESSONS IN LOVE"		1.00	1.00		Extracts
	"GOT A FUNNY FEELING"		2.00	2.55		taken from
	"THE YOUNG ONES"		2.55	6.00		
	WE SAY YEAH		7.50	10.40		

MACHINE No. ST 18
STUDIO Kingston ABC.
TAPE LENGTH 2400 FT.
TAPE SPEED 15
TAPE TYPE 477
RECORDING ENGINEER MN/KNT
DATE 7TH MARCH 1962

PLEASE RETURN TO TAPE LIBRARY

Tape box showing part of Cliff's set, recorded live at the ABC Theatre, Kingston, 7 March 1962, but still unreleased.

Inter-departmental MEMORANDUM   Date   5th April 1962

To   Mr. E. Fowler,   c/S8.NWP/FG
     Abbey Road.   Mr. H. Hack,
                        Abbey Road.

Re: CLIFF RICHARD AND THE SHADOWS – KINGSTON L.P.

      I should be grateful if you could supply as soon as possible
flat transfer Mono lacquers of the equalised and compressed tape
of the above.   This is very urgent and any hold-up would delay
the release of this potentially fast moving record.

                              NORRIE PARAMOR
                              E.M.I. Records Ltd.

RECEIVED
-6 APR 1962
STUDIOS LTD.

Documentation relating to live recordings made at the ABC Theatre, Kingston, 7 March 1962, but still unreleased.

To MATRIX DEPT.
Mr. PARAMOR Date 9-4-62

Please receive the undermentioned LACQUER ORIGINALS
from ABBEY RD STUDIOS Room 24

Serial Nos:

2 NON PROCESS LACQUERS

"THE CLIFF RICHARD SHOW LP.

SIDE 1. THE SHADOWS
SIDE 2. CLIFF RICHARD

MONO

2 × 1236

Ref 1736D

ABBEY ROAD STUDIOS

live album of Cliff and the Shadows on tour, Columbia taped the first and second houses at the ABC Theatre, Kingston, on 7 March. However, information on the tape box indicates a number of technical faults, particularly distortion and level changes probably due to the conditions under which it was recorded although these were remedied at a later date when a copy tape was made from the first house versions, as the tapes for the second house have been heavily cut and edited. It is known that EMI still possesses tapes containing completely finished album sides of the Shadows set on side 1, and Cliff's on side 2, showing that Columbia were at the time well advanced with their plans for the CLIFF RICHARD SHOW album. A tantalising piece of information about these recordings is that Cliff performed a number of songs that were never recorded in the studio. Of these were a great rocker *Dim, Dim The Lights*, the country orientated *Rovin' Gambler*, the rousing gospel treatment of *Save My Soul* and the R & B classic *I Got A Woman*. When the idea of the album was dropped, attention shifted towards the production of the SUMMER HOLIDAY soundtrack. Work began in April, and continued at a series of recording dates through to November, producing such classics as *Summer Holiday, The Next Time, Bachelor*

Boy and *Dancing Shoes*. Not all the sessions during this period were restricted to soundtrack recordings, and some other material was taped. Of these, the reworking of the Jerry Lee Lewis hit *It'll Be Me* was the most successful, providing Columbia with an obvious choice for a single release. As usual, all the sessions took place in studio 2 at Abbey Road with the regular Shadows line-up. There was only one change, from the 5 May recording date, when Jet Harris left, and his place was taken by Brian Locking. For the August and November soundtrack sessions the Stanley Black Orchestra provided the orchestral arrangements, and the Mike Sammes Singers the vocal backing on the production numbers.

April 1963 saw Cliff back in the recording studios again. However, the location had changed from Abbey Road to EMI's studio in Barcelona, Spain. During four nights, a total of 12 tracks were laid down that would become the first foreign language album WHEN IN SPAIN. Overdubbing of the Norrie Paramor Strings and backing vocals by Bruce Welch and Cliff were carried out at Abbey Road's studio 2 between 14 and 28 May. In August more foreign recordings were taped; this time the setting was the Jubilee Hall in Blackpool. The songs Cliff was to record were a collection of popular French hits. *J'Attendrai* and *C'est Si Bon* had both enjoyed chart success in France and *La Mer* and *Boum* were two of the most famous songs from the pen of the great Charles Trenet. These four tracks found their way onto the WHEN IN FRANCE EP. The next few sessions were aimed at producing new singles and the first material for the WONDERFUL LIFE soundtrack album.

EMI Tape Review of live recordings made at the ABC Theatre, Kingston, 7 March 1962, but still unreleased.

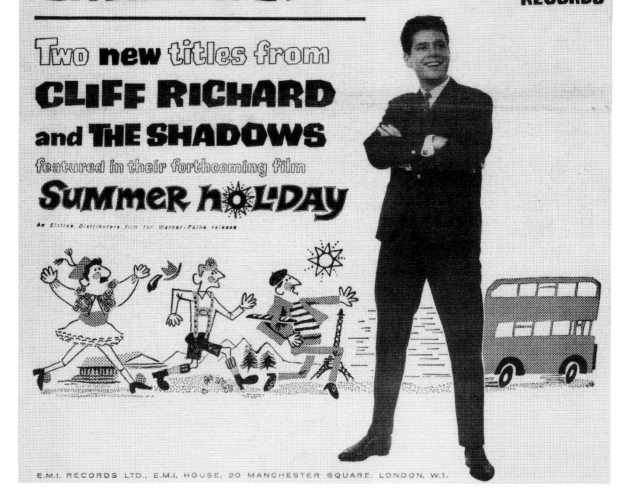

Studio session for Columbia
18 January 1962
Abbey Road

| 08 | Turn Around | 32 Minutes And 17 Seconds |
| — | I'm On My Way | 32 Minutes And 17 Seconds |

The Norrie Paramor Orchestra
The Mike Sammes Singers

Producer: Norrie Paramor
Engineer: Malcolm Addy
Recorded in studio 2
Session hours: 7.00 pm–10.30 pm

Live recordings for Columbia
7 March 1962
ABC, Kingston, Surrey

—	*Apache–Shazam*	*Unissued*
—	*Shadoogie*	*Unissued*
—	*Wonderful Land*	*Unissued*
—	*All My Sorrows*	*Unissued*
—	*Quarter To Three*	*Unissued*
—	*Nivram*	*Unissued*
—	*Little B*	*Unissued*
—	*FBI*	*Unissued*
—	*Do You Wanna Dance*	*Unissued*
—	*Dim Dim The Lights*	*Unissued*
—	*My Blue Heaven*	*Unissued*
—	*Razzle Dazzle*	*Unissued*
—	*Rovin' Gambler*	*Unissued*
—	*Save My Soul*	*Unissued*
—	*When The Girl In Your Arms*	*Unissued*
—	*I Gotta Woman*	*Unissued*
—	*The Young Ones Medley*	*Unissued*

Do You Wanna Dance. Live at Kingston, 7 March 1962.

Guitars: Hank Marvin
       Bruce Welch
Bass: Jet Harris
Drums: Brian Bennett

Producer: Norrie Paramor
Engineers: Malcolm Addy / Ken Townsend
Session hours: 6.30 pm–11.00 pm

The first eight tracks feature the Shadows only.

The first and second houses were recorded but as the tracks were exactly the same only one house is listed here.

The Young Ones Medley consists of Lessons In Love / Got A Funny Feeling / The Young Ones / We Say Yeah.

Studio session for Columbia
4 April 1962
Abbey Road

| 07 | For You For Me | Holiday Carnival EP |
| 06 | Walking The Blues | 32 Minutes And 17 Seconds |

Guitars: Hank Marvin
       Bruce Welch
Bass: Jet Harris
Drums: Brian Bennett

Producer: Norrie Paramor
Engineer: Malcolm Addy
Recorded in studio 2
Session hours: 7.00 pm–10.30 pm

Studio session for Columbia
5 April 1962
Abbey Road

| — | *Summer Holiday* | *Unissued* |

Guitars: Hank Marvin
       Bruce Welch
Bass: Jet Harris
Drums: Brian Bennett

Producer: Norrie Paramor
Engineer: Malcolm Addy
Recorded in studio 2
Session hours: 7.00 pm–10.30 pm

Studio session for Columbia
12 April 1962
Abbey Road

| — | *Dancing Shoes* | *Unissued* |

Guitars: Hank Marvin
       Bruce Welch
Bass: Jet Harris
Drums: Brian Bennett

Producer: Norrie Paramor
Engineer: Malcolm Addy
Recorded in studio 2
Session hours: 7.00 pm–10.30 pm

Studio session for Columbia
1 May 1962
Abbey Road

| 30 | Take Special Care | Cliff Richard |
| — | *I'll Be Waiting* | *Unissued* |

Guitars: Hank Marvin
       Bruce Welch
Bass: Jet Harris
Drums: Brian Bennett

Producer: Norrie Paramor
Engineer: Malcolm Addy
Recorded in studio 2
Session hours: 7.00 pm–10.00 pm

Studio session for Columbia
5 May 1962
Abbey Road

| 04 | Dancing Shoes | B-side |
| 11 | Summer Holiday | A-side |

Guitars: Hank Marvin
       Bruce Welch
Bass: Brian Locking
Drums: Brian Bennett

Producer: Norrie Paramor
Engineer: Malcolm Addy
Recorded in studio 2
Session hours: 7.00 pm–10.45 pm

These two tracks are listed as remakes on the EMI session sheets.

Studio session for Columbia
10 May 1962
Abbey Road

09   The Next Time   A-side
—   *Quarter To Three*   *Unissued*

Guitars: Hank Marvin
        Bruce Welch
Bass: Brian Locking
Drums: Brian Bennett
Piano / Organ: Norrie Paramor

Producer: Norrie Paramor
Engineer: Malcolm Addy
Recorded in studio 2
Session hours: 7.00 pm – 10.30 pm

Studio session for Columbia
17 May 1962
Abbey Road

—   When My Dreamboat Comes
    Home   32 Minutes And 17 Seconds

—   Blueberry Hill   32 Minutes And 17 Seconds

—   It'll Be Me   A-side

Guitars: Hank Marvin
        Bruce Welch
Bass: Brian Locking
Drums: Brian Bennett

Producer: Norrie Paramor
Engineer: Malcolm Addy
Recorded in studio 2
Session hours: 7.00 pm – 11.00 pm

Studio session for Columbia
12 July 1962
Abbey Road

11   A Forever Kind Of Love   Forever Kind Of Love EP
sp   Razzle Dazzle   Cliff Richard
03   Reelin' and Rockin'   Cliff Richard

Guitars: Hank Marvin
        Bruce Welch
Bass: Brian Locking
Drums: Brian Bennett
The Norrie Paramor Orchestra

Producer: Norrie Paramor
Engineer: Peter Bown
Recorded in studio 2
Session hours: 7.00 pm – 10.45 pm

Razzle Dazzle is an edit of takes 1 and 4.

Studio session for Columbia
20 July 1962
Abbey Road

14   *Wonderful To Be Young*   *Unissued*
12   *Sweet Dreams*   *Unissued*

Guitars: Hank Marvin
        Bruce Welch
Bass: Brian Locking
Drums: Brian Bennett

Producer: Norrie Paramor
Engineers: Malcolm Addy / Peter Vince
Recorded in studio 2
Session hours: 7.00 pm – 10.30 pm

Studio session for Columbia
11 August 1962
Abbey Road

28   It's Wonderful To Be Young   A-side (US)

Guitars: Hank Marvin
        Bruce Welch
Bass: Brian Locking
Drums: Brian Bennett

Producer: Norrie Paramor
Engineer: Malcolm Addy
Recorded in studio 1
Session hours: 1.00 am – 4.45 am

MONO/STEREO   4 TRACK REMIX TO MONO   **RECORDING SHEET**   Date of Session 27ᵗʰ Aug 1962   Job No: 3854/ P069/

Sheet: _____ of: _____ Class: _____   Overall Title _____

ARTISTIC INFORMATION								COSTING INFORMATION			
ARTISTE(S) AND/OR CAST		CONDUCTOR						MATERIALS USED	2 x 77	ORDER NUMBER	
		ORCHESTRA						SESSION BOOKED TIME	10 – 12	COMPANY	Columbia
		ACCOMPANIMENT						SESSION ACTUAL	10 – 1	STUDIO/CONTROL ROOM	1 / 1A
		ART. DEPT. REP.						SET-UP/PLAYBACK	½ hr.	ENGINEERS	HA/CN/A·

TITLES and MATRIX Nos.	AUTHOR/COMPOSER/ PUBLISHER	REEL NUMBERS	FALSE STARTS	TAKE No.	TAKE DETAILS FROM	TAKE DETAILS TO	DUR.	M	REMARKS
CLIFF RICHARD									
"ALL AT ONCE"		E47728		6	Complete		3·48	M	
"A SWINGIN' AFFAIR"	ED/M	10	>	7	m			M	Equalised
				8				M	& compress
				9				M	
" TAKE YOU FOR A RIDE"	ED/m.		(9) >	8				M	when
				13				M	edited
				20			4·37	M	
"A STRANGER IN TOWN"	ED/m		(13) >	4	m			M	Transfer
				1			2·34	M	flat
"YUGOSLAV WEDDING"			(2) >	3	m			M	
				5				M	
				6			2·56	M	
	ED/m								

Recording sheets showing 4-track remix to mono of "Summer Holiday" soundtracks.

MONO/STEREO   REMIX FROM 4 TRACK to MONO & STEREO.   **RECORDING SHEET**   Date of Session 19-11-62   Job No: P0184CM

Sheet: _____ of: _____ Class: *Popular*   Overall Title _____

ARTISTIC INFORMATION								COSTING INFORMATION			
ARTISTE(S) AND/OR CAST	Cliff Richard and The Shadows	CONDUCTOR						MATERIALS USED	1 x 77	ORDER NUMBER	
		ORCHESTRA						SESSION BOOKED TIME	10 – 1 pm	COMPANY	Columbia
		ACCOMPANIMENT						SESSION ACTUAL	11·45 – 1·30	STEREO/CONTROL ROOM	2/1A
		ART. DEPT. REP.	N PARAMOR					SET-UP/PLAYBACK		ENGINEERS	MA RL

TITLES and MATRIX Nos.	AUTHOR/COMPOSER/ PUBLISHER	REEL NUMBERS	FALSE STARTS	TAKE No.	TAKE DETAILS FROM	TAKE DETAILS TO	DUR.	M	REMARKS
"Bachelor Boy"		E48320Z		11	Complete			(M)	MONO &
"Big News"				13	Complete			(M)	STEREO
All at once				7	Complete		3·48	(M)	STEREO ONLY

Film soundtrack recordings for
Summer Holiday
26 August 1962
Abbey Road

—	Yugoslav Wedding	Summer Holiday
—	Take You For A Ride	Summer Holiday
04	Stranger In Town	Summer Holiday
–	Swingin' Affair	Summer Holiday
sp	All At Once	Summer Holiday

The Mike Sammes Singers
The Stanley Black Orchestra

Producer: Norrie Paramor
Engineers: Malcolm Addy / Richard Langham
Recorded in studio 2
Session hours: 2.30 pm–5.30 pm and
7.00 pm–10.00 pm

All At Once is an edit of takes 6 and 7.

Film soundtrack recordings for
Summer Holiday
16 November 1962
Abbey Road

sp	Big News	Summer Holiday
sp	Bachelor Boy	B-side

Guitars: Hank Marvin
         Bruce Welch
Bass: Brian Locking
Drums: Brian Bennett

Producer: Norrie Paramor
Engineer: Malcolm Addy
Recorded in studio 2
Session hours: 7.00 pm–11.00 pm

Big News is an edit of takes 12 and 13.

Bachelor Boy is an edit of takes 10 and 11.

Film soundtrack recordings for
Summer Holiday
22 November 1962
Abbey Road

05	Orlando's Mime – Part 1	Summer Holiday
07	Orlando's Mime – Part 2	Summer Holiday
12	Orlando's Mime – Part 3	Summer Holiday
05	Really Waltzing – Part 1	Summer Holiday
09	Really Waltzing – Part 2	Summer Holiday
06	Opening – Part 1	Summer Holiday
09	Opening – Part 2	Summer Holiday
—	Seven Days To Our Holiday	Summer Holiday

The Stanley Black Orchestra
The Mike Sammes Singers

Producer: Norrie Paramor
Engineer: Malcolm Addy
Recorded in studio 2
Session hours: 7.00 pm–10.30 pm

Orlando's Mime and Opening are orchestral tracks only.

Studio session for Columbia
6 December 1962
Abbey Road

sp	Carnival	Holiday Carnival EP
04	I'm In The Mood	Love Songs EP
02	Where The Four Winds Blow	Why Don't They Understand EP

The Norrie Paramor Orchestra
The Mike Sammes Singers

Producer: Norrie Paramor
Engineers: Malcolm Addy / Peter Vince
Recorded in studio 2
Session hours: 7.00 pm–9.45 pm

Carnival is an edit of takes 3 and 6.

Studio session for Columbia
12 December 1962
Abbey Road

04	I Found A Rose	Love Is Forever
03	Moonlight Bay	Holiday Carnival EP
04	Some Of These Days	Holiday Carnival EP

The Norrie Paramor Orchestra
The Mike Sammes Singers

Producer: Norrie Paramor
Engineers: Malcolm Addy / Peter Vince
Recorded in studio 2
Session hours: 7.00 pm–9.30 pm

Studio session for Columbia
21 December 1962
Abbey Road

04	Perfidia	Cliff Richard

Guitars: Hank Marvin
         Bruce Welch
Bass: Brian Locking
Drums: Brian Bennett

Producer: Norrie Paramor
Engineer: Malcolm Addy
Recorded in studio 2
Session hours: 7.00 pm–10.00 pm

This is an English version of the song Cliff would eventually record in Spanish for the When In Spain album.

Studio session for Columbia
28 December 1962
Abbey Road

03	It's All In The Game	A-side
08	*From This Day On*	*Unissued*
06	I Only Have Eyes For You	Love Songs

The Norrie Paramor Orchestra
The Mike Sammes Singers

Producer: Norrie Paramor
Engineer: Malcolm Addy
Recorded in studio 2
Session hours: 2.30 pm–5.30 pm

Studio session for Columbia
8 March 1963
Abbey Road

06	Lucky Lips	A-side
09	I Wonder	B-side

Guitars: Hank Marvin
         Bruce Welch
Bass: Brian Locking
Drums: Brian Bennett

Cover for sheet music of *Lucky Lips*.

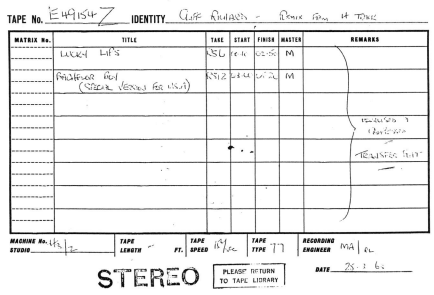

TAPE No. E49154Z   IDENTITY Cliff Richard – Remix from 4 Track

MATRIX No.	TITLE	TAKE	START	FINISH	MASTER	REMARKS
	LUCKY LIPS	RS6	00.16	02.56	M	
	BACHELOR BOY (SPECIAL VERSION FOR USA)	RS12	03.46	05.20	M	
						RELEASED ? Christmas
						TRANSFER FLAT

MACHINE No. 43/2   STUDIO _____   TAPE LENGTH _____ FT.   TAPE SPEED 15/sec   TAPE TYPE 77   RECORDING ENGINEER MA/ec   DATE 25.3.63

STEREO   PLEASE RETURN TO TAPE LIBRARY

Tape box showing the special version of *Bachelor Boy* for the US market.

Producer: Norrie Paramor
Engineer: Malcolm Addy
Recorded in studio 2
Session hours: 7.00 pm–10.45 pm

Studio session for Columbia
10 April 1963
Abbey Road

10   Your Eyes Tell On You   B-side

Guitars: Hank Marvin
            Bruce Welch
Bass: Brian Locking
Drums: Brian Bennett

Producer: Norrie Paramor
Engineer: Malcolm Addy
Recorded in studio 2
Session hours: 6.30 pm–9.15 pm

Studio session for Columbia
28 April 1963
Barcelona

07   Perfidia   When In Spain
05   Frenesi   When In Spain
23   Tus Besos   When In Spain
04   Amor, Amor, Amor   When In Spain

Guitars: Hank Marvin
            Bruce Welch
Bass: Brian Locking
Drums: Brian Bennett
The Norrie Paramor Strings

Producer: Norrie Paramor
Engineer: Malcolm Addy
Session hours: 6.00 pm–9.00 pm

**Studio session for Columbia
29 April 1963
Barcelona**

13	Solamente Una Vez	When In Spain
13	Quizas, Quizas, Quizas	When In Spain
05	Carnival	When In Spain
14	Quien Sera	When In Spain

Guitars: Hank Marvin
        Bruce Welch
Bass: Brian Locking
Drums: Brian Bennett
The Norrie Paramor Strings

Producer: Norrie Paramor
Engineer: Malcolm Addy
Session hours: 7.00 pm–10.00 pm

**Studio session for Columbia
30 April 1963
Barcelona**

15	Te Quiero Dijeste	When In Spain
09	Vaya Con Dios	When In Spain
07	Me Lo Dijo Adela	When In Spain

Guitars: Hank Marvin
        Bruce Welch
Bass: Brian Locking
Drums: Brian Bennett
The Norrie Paramor Strings

Producer: Norrie Paramor
Engineer: Malcolm Addy
Session hours: 6.00 pm–10.00 pm

**Studio session for Columbia
1 May 1963
Barcelona**

11	Maria No Mas	When In Spain

Guitars: Hank Marvin
        Bruce Welch
Bass: Brian Locking
Drums: Brian Bennett
The Norrie Paramor Strings

Producer: Norrie Paramor
Engineer: Malcolm Addy
Session hours: 7.00 pm–10.00 pm

**Studio session for Columbia
5 August 1963
Jubilee Hall Blackpool**

10	Boum	When In France EP
08	La Mer	When In France EP
—	*J'Attendrai*	*Unissued*
12	C'est Si Bon	When In France EP

Guitars: Hank Marvin
        Bruce Welch
Bass: Brian Locking
Drums: Brian Bennett

Producer: Norrie Paramor
Engineer: Malcolm Addy
Session hours: midday–4.00 pm

**Studio session for Columbia
6 August 1963
Jubilee Hall Blackpool**

10	J'Attendrai	When In France EP
—	Say You're Mine	B-side

Guitars: Hank Marvin
        Bruce Welch
Bass: Brian Locking
Drums: Brian Bennett

Producer: Norrie Paramor
Engineer: Malcolm Addy
Session hours: midday–4.00 pm

2 TRK

TAPE No. _E50290_   IDENTITY _CLIFF RICHARD AND THE SHADOWS_

MATRIX No.	TITLE	TAKE	START	FINISH	MASTER	REMARKS
--------	BOOM [TRACK 2]	7	0020	0210		
--------	BOUM	8				
--------		9	0240	0440		
--------		10	0450	0650	(M)	1·54

--------	J'ATTENDRAI ~~TRACE~~	8	0700	0720		

--------	C'EST SI BON [TRACK 2]		0730	1000	Test.	
--------		11	1010	1050		
--------		(12)	1100	1270	(M)	be edited.
--------						2·03

1380

MACHINE No. _STiB_   TAPE LENGTH   FT.   TAPE SPEED _15_   TAPE TYPE _77_   RECORDING ENGINEER _M.A._
STUDIO _JUBILEE HALL_
BLACKPOOL   DATE _5 AUGUST 63_

THIS TAPE IS NOT SUITABLE FOR TRANSFER

Tape box of foreign language recordings for the WHEN IN FRANCE EP. Note the comments on the unsuitability for transfer.

Studio session for Columbia
9 August 1963
Jubilee Hall Blackpool

| 10 | What've I Gotta Do | Wonderful Life |

Guitars: Hank Marvin
        Bruce Welch
Bass: Brian Locking
Drums: Brian Bennett

Producer: Norrie Paramor
Engineer: Malcolm Addy
Session hours: midday–4.00 pm

Studio session for Columbia
11 August 1963
Abbey Road

| — | Rote Lippen Soll Man Küssen (Lucky Lips) | German A-side |

Producer: Norrie Paramor
Engineer: Malcolm Addy
Recorded in studio 3
Session hours: 7.00 pm–9.15 pm

Cliff's vocals were dubbed onto the existing track of Lucky Lips for this foreign release.

Studio session for Columbia
13 October 1963
Abbey Road

| 11 | Don't Talk To Him | A-side |

Guitars: Hank Marvin
        Bruce Welch
Bass: Brian Locking
Drums: Brian Bennett

Producer: Norrie Paramor
Engineer: Malcolm Addy
Recorded in studio 3
Session hours: 7.00 pm–10.30 pm

**Film soundtrack recordings for
Wonderful Life
1 November 1963
Abbey Road**

16	Do You Remember	Wonderful Life

Guitars: Hank Marvin
         Bruce Welch
Bass: Brian Locking
Drums: Brian Bennett

Producer: Norrie Paramor
Engineer: Malcolm Addy
Recorded in studio 3
Session hours: 7.00 pm–10.45 pm

**Film soundtrack recordings for
Wonderful Life
5 November 1963
Abbey Road**

18	Wonderful Life	Wonderful Life
11	On The Beach	A-side

Guitars: Hank Marvin
         Bruce Welch
Bass: Brian Locking
Drums: Brian Bennett

Producer: Norrie Paramor
Engineer: Malcolm Addy
Recorded in studio 3
Session hours: 7.00 pm–10.45 pm

**Studio session for Columbia
8 November 1963
Abbey Road**

—	*Look Don't Touch*	*Unissued*

Guitars: Hank Marvin
         Bruce Welch
Bass: Brian Locking
Drums: Brian Bennett

Producer: Norrie Paramor
Engineer: Malcolm Addy
Recorded in studio 3
Session hours: 7.00 pm–10.00 pm

**Film soundtrack recordings for
Wonderful Life
10 November 1963
Abbey Road**

—	A Matter Of Moments	Wonderful Life

Guitars: Hank Marvin
         Bruce Welch
Bass: Brian Locking
Drums: Brian Bennett

Producer: Norrie Paramor
Engineer: Malcolm Addy
Recorded in studio 2
Session hours: 7.00 pm–10.00 pm

**Studio session for Columbia
17 November 1963
Abbey Road**

—	I Only Came To Say Goodbye	Angel EP
—	Constantly (L'Edera)	A-side
—	*I Only Know I Love You*	*Unissued*

The Norrie Paramor Orchestra
Drums: Brian Bennett

Producer: Norrie Paramor
Engineer: Malcolm Addy
Recorded in studio 2
Session hours: 7.00 pm–10.15 pm

**Studio session for Columbia
23 November 1963
Abbey Road**

—	Watch What You Do With My Baby	B-side
—	I'm The Lonely One	A-side

Guitar: Hank Marvin
Bass: John Rostill
Drums: Brian Bennett

Producer: Norrie Paramor
Engineer: Malcolm Addy
Recorded in studio 2
Session hours: 7.00 pm–10.30 pm

4

Wonderful Life

1964–1965

───────────── **The Records** ─────────────

I'm The Lonely One /
  Watch What You Do With
  My Baby
	Single	8/—

Constantly / True, True Lovin'	Single	3/—
On The Beach / A Matter of Moments	Single	7/—
The Twelfth Of Never / I'm Afraid To Go Home	Single	8/—
I Could Easily Fall (In Love With You) / I'm In Love	Single	9/—
The Minute You're Gone / Just Another Guy	Single	1/—
On My Word / Just A Little Bit Too Late	Single	12/—
The Time In Between / Look Before You Love	Single	22/—
Wind Me Up / In The Night	Single	2/—
When In France	EP	
Cliff Sings Don't Talk To Him	EP	15
Cliff's Palladium Successes	EP	
Wonderful Life	EP	3
A Forever Kind Of Love	EP	
Wonderful Life No. 2	EP	
Hits From Wonderful Life	EP	
Why Don't They Understand	EP	
Cliff Hits From 'Aladdin And His Wonderful Lamp'	EP	20
Look In My Eyes Maria	EP	15
Angel	EP	
Take Four	EP	4

EP chart positions taken from 'Record Retailer'

Wonderful Life	LP	2
Aladdin And His Wonderful Lamp	LP	13
Cliff Richard	LP	9
More Hits By Cliff	LP	20

When In Rome	LP	
Love Is Forever	LP	19

As Beatlemania began to develop into a phenomenon, Columbia released *I'm The Lonely One* as the 1964 new year single, thereby kicking off to a good start with the single reaching the top ten. At the same time, *Don't Talk To Him*, the smash hit from 1963, re-entered the chart for one week at number 50. For the follow up, an adaptation of the old Italian hit song *L'Edera* was chosen, and did even better, appearing at number 3 as *Constantly*. The next single *On The Beach* was the lead and only single from the WONDERFUL LIFE soundtrack, and though still a strong release chartwise, it showed a slight decline when compared to its predecessors. The single

A rare EP sleeve from Europe.

I Could Easily Fall, taken from the cast recording of Cliff's pantomime ALADDIN AND HIS WONDERFUL LAMP, was already well on the way to becoming a hit before the show opened at the London Palladium just before Christmas 1964. But by far the big sellers of this period were those resulting from the first studio sessions in Nashville and New York. *The Minute You're Gone* and *Wind Me Up* reached number 1 and 2 respectively.

The albums represented a mixed bag indeed. In the soundtrack division, WONDERFUL LIFE attained the best chart placing at number 2, not having such a wide appeal as SUMMER HOLIDAY, while the ALADDIN set did not do quite so well, only peaking at number 13. In the pop division CLIFF RICHARD consisted of leftovers from various sessions over a period of three years, and fared slightly better chartwise. MORE HITS BY CLIFF proved not to be quite as strong as CLIFF'S HIT ALBUM. It only reached the number 20 spot, and only for one week. Even worse was Cliff's last complete album of foreign-language recordings. WHEN IN ROME failed to register on the chart at all, but the final album of the year, LOVE IS FOREVER, showed a considerable improvement by reaching number 19, although like MORE HITS only remained on the chart for one week.

No fewer than twelve EPs were released during this period following a by now predictable pattern of recycling material from albums. WONDERFUL LIFE No. 1 was the most successful of these despite the fact that the four tracks on the EP were also on the major hit album.

Cliff at his Savile Row London office. Early sixties.

Collectors' Notes

The track from the ALADDIN cast album *This Was My Special Day* was issued as a theatre-only single not available through the usual record outlets, but only in the foyer of the London Palladium during the run of the pantomime. The single featured Cliff sharing vocals with other cast members: Audrey Bayley, Joan Palethorpe and Faye Fisher, and was given a regular Columbia catalogue number of DB 7435.

The May 1965 sessions produced an unreleased song. *Deep Purple* was recently discovered on a single-sided 7″ Emidisc acetate lasting 2 minutes and 10 seconds. It is unknown how many copies exist, but one was included in the Rock 'n' Roll Memorabilia Auction at Sotheby's on 28 August 1986.

Last but not least, there's of course the *Angel/Razzle Dazzle* single (Columbia DC 762), that like the previous ones had been pressed in the UK for distribution overseas, and had found its way briefly into UK record outlets.

The Sessions

Studio sessions for Columbia: Abbey Road
Wonderful Life soundtrack sessions:
 Abbey Road
Studio sessions for Columbia: Nashville
Studio sessions for Columbia: New York
Studio sessions for Columbia: EMI Lisbon
Aladdin cast sessions: Abbey Road

The first 1964 soundtrack session was done for WONDERFUL LIFE with one vital change in the recording procedure – whereas before the soundtrack sessions had been live ones, now first a basic track of the music would be taped and Cliff's vocals and back-up vocals would be dubbed in later. As the film called for plenty of songs, a slew of material was taped and 14 songs eventually found their way onto the soundtrack album. The Stanley Black Orchestra and the Mike Sammes Singers swelled the ranks of the regulars.

In August, twelve regular studio recordings were done, and all of these took place in Nashville and New York. Although not much is known about the sessions, it is certain that the Jordanaires were called in for vocal support, being featured alongside a number of session musicians. A new producer entered the studios with Cliff for the tracks recorded in Nashville – Billy Sherrill. Later Sherrill was to build on his reputation through a string of solid hits by country artists like Tammy Wynette and

impressive work with, among others, the British rock singer Elvis Costello. Of the material recorded, a great number of songs were of a very high quality indeed as proven by the three hit singles – *On My Word*, *The Minute You're Gone* and *Wind Me Up*. Plans were made to follow up the overall successful American recording sessions with some more at the EMI Lisbon studios in October, when Cliff taped an entire session in two days of Italian language recordings over pre-recorded backing tapes that comprised the material for the commercially unsuccessful WHEN IN ROME album.

The taping of the songs for the ALADDIN pantomime cast album was done later that month at Abbey Road at a soundtrack session with the musical score by the Shadows, and Cliff sharing vocals on a number of tracks with other cast members – Una Stubbs, Joan Palethorpe and Audrey Bayley were brought in for the sessions on the 16th.

On the sessions for KINDA LATIN, three different orchestras were employed to provide the Latin setting of the material that was to be recorded, and veered more towards straight middle-of-the-road repertoire.

In all probability the last session of the year was set up to record an album of Walt Disney songs. Four songs were taped before the projected album was dropped and it was decided to shelve these recordings.

Studio session for Columbia
20 March 1964
Abbey Road

— Zuviel Allein
 (I'm The Lonely One) German release

— Sag 'No' Zu Ihm
 (Don't Talk To Him) German release

Producer: Norrie Paramor
Engineer: —
Recorded in studio 2
Session hours: 7.00 pm–10.00 pm

Cliff's vocals were dubbed onto the existing tracks for this foreign release.

Studio session for Columbia
26 March 1964
Abbey Road

— True, True Lovin' B-side
— *Just A Little Bit Too Late* *Unissued*

Guitars: Hank Marvin
 Bruce Welch
Bass: John Rostill
Drums: Brian Bennett

Producer: Norrie Paramor
Engineer: —
Recorded in studio 2
Session hours: 7.00 pm–9.30 pm

**Film soundtrack recordings for
Wonderful Life
22 April 1964
Abbey Road**

—	In The Stars	Wonderful Life
—	A Little Imagination	Wonderful Life
—	Home	Wonderful Life
—	All Kinds Of People	Wonderful Life

The Stanley Black Orchestra
The Mike Sammes Singers

Producer: Norrie Paramor
Engineer: —
Recorded in studio 2
Session hours: 7.00 pm–10.00 pm

**Film soundtrack recordings for
Wonderful Life
20 May 1964
Abbey Road**

05	We Love A Movie	Wonderful Life
02	Youth And Experience – Part 1	Wonderful Life
04	Youth And Experience – Part 2	Wonderful Life
18	*Wonderful Life*	*Unissued*
02	A Girl In Every Port – Part 1	Wonderful Life
03	A Girl In Every Port – Part 2	Wonderful Life
—	A Girl In Every Port – Part 3	Wonderful Life

The Stanley Black Orchestra

Producer: Bob Barratt
Engineers: Malcolm Addy / Alan Kane
Recorded in studio 2
Session hours: 7.00 pm–10.00 pm

On the EMI session sheets these are listed as backing tracks only.

**Film soundtrack recordings for
Wonderful Life
26 May 1964
Abbey Road**

05	Youth And Experience	Wonderful Life
sp	A Girl In Every Port	Wonderful Life
05	We Love A Movie	Wonderful Life

The Mike Sammes Singers

Producer: Norrie Paramor
Engineers: Malcolm Addy / Richard Langham
Recorded in studio 2
Session hours: 7.00 pm–9.30 pm

This session was for the superimposition of vocals onto the 20 May backing tracks.

**Studio session for Columbia
23 June 1964
Abbey Road**

sp	Twelfth Of Never	A-side
06	My Colouring Book	Love Is Forever EP
sp	Maria	Look In My Eyes Maria EP

The Norrie Paramor Orchestra
The Mike Sammes Singers

Producer: Norrie Paramor
Engineer: Malcolm Addy
Recorded in studio 2
Session hours: 7.00 pm–10.00 pm

Twelfth Of Never is an edit of takes 3 and 4.

Maria is an edit of takes 7 and 8.

**Studio session for Columbia
17 July 1964
Abbey Road**

04	It's Not For Me To Say	Cliff Richard
04	*The Song From Moulin Rouge*	*Unissued*

RECORDING SHEET

MONO/STEREO

Sheet: 1 of: ___ Class: Popular Overall Title: REMIX FROM 4 TRACK Date of Session 27-5-64 3775 Job No: 4CMS

ARTISTIC INFORMATION		COSTING INFORMATION	

ARTISTE(S) AND/OR CAST: Cliff Richard

CONDUCTOR: S. BLACK
ORCHESTRA: — " —
ACCOMPANIMENT: —
ART. DEPT. REP.: N. PARAMOR

MATERIALS USED: 1 x 77 ORDER NUMBER: —
SESSION BOOKED TIME: 10 — 1 COMPANY: COLUMBIA
SESSION ACTUAL: 10 — 1 STUDIO CONTROL ROOM: 2 — 1B
SET-UP/PLAYBACK: ½ ENGINEERS: MA DJL

TITLES and Matrix Nos.	AUTHOR/COMPOSER/PUBLISHER	REEL NUMBERS	FALSE STARTS	TAKE No.	FROM	TO	DUR.	BEST	REMARKS
WONDERFUL LIFE		ES2874		Rm2	INTRO			B	
				Rm3	COMPLETE			B	
A GIRL IN EVERY PORT				RM1	1ST PART			B	
				RM	2nd — " —			B	
HOME				RM1	COMPLETE			B	
				Rm2	EDIT PIECE			B	EQUALISED
A LITTLE IMAGINATION				RM1	COMPLETE			B	
IN THE STARS				RM1	— " —			B	AND
WE LOVE A MOVIE				RM1	— " —			B	
ALL KINDS OF PEOPLE				RM1	1ST PART			R	COMPRESSED
				Rm2	2nd PART			B	
YOUTH AND EXPERIENCE				RM1	COMPLETE			B	TRANSFER FLAT.

Ref. 9864

Recording sheet showing remix from 4-track of WONDERFUL LIFE session.

Mr. BOB BARRATT Columbia P066 4CM

TAPE No. E 533527 IDENTITY CLIFF RICHARD acc dir NORRIE PARAMOR

MATRIX No.	TITLE	TAKE	START	FINISH	MASTER	REMARKS
	Song from "MOULIN ROUGE"	1	0·12	2·24	2·15	Tr. 1. Rhythm
		2	F/S			2. strings
		3	2·49	5·13	2·24	3. choir
		4	5·31	7·55	BEST 2·22	4. Vocal
	LOOK HOMEWARD, ANGEL	1	8·13	11·00	2·45	
		2	11·23	14·13	BEST 2·50	
	IT'S NOT FOR ME TO SAY	1	14·39	17·44	3·04	
		2	18·31	B/D		Continued on E 533534

MACHINE No. M10 N°2/1B
STUDIO: ___
TAPE LENGTH: ___
FT.: ___
TAPE SPEED: 15 ips
TAPE TYPE: 888
RECORDING ENGINEER: MA AB
DATE: 17th July 1964

02	Look Homeward Angel	Love Is Forever
sp	All Of A Sudden My Heart Sings	Love Is Forever
—	Sway	Cliff Richard
—	Magic Is The Moonlight	Cliff Richard
—	You Belong To My Heart	Cliff Richard

The Norrie Paramor Orchestra
The Mike Sammes Singers

Producer: Norrie Paramor
Engineer: Malcolm Addy
Recorded in studio 2
Session hours: 7.00 pm–9.45 pm

All Of A Sudden My Heart Sings is an edit of takes 5 and 7.

Studio session for Columbia
24 July 1964
Abbey Road

—	Where Is Your Heart	Look In My Eyes Maria EP
—	Why Don't They Understand	Why Don't They Understand EP
—	House Without Windows	Cliff Richard
—	I'm Afraid To Go Home	B-side

The Norrie Paramor Orchestra
The Mike Sammes Singers

Producer: Norrie Paramor
Engineer: —
Recorded in studio 2
Session hours: 7.00 pm–10.45 pm

Studio session for Columbia
19 August 1964
Nashville

| 08 | On My Word | A-side |
| 08 | My Heart Is An Open Book | Take Four EP |

Acetate for personal use.

07	Lies And Kisses	Take Four EP
09	Again	Cliff Richard
07	Look In My Eyes Maria	Look In My Eyes Maria EP
11	Paradise Lost	Love Is Forever

Musicians: —
Vocals: The Jordanaires

Producer: Billy Sherrill
Engineer: —
Session hours: —

Studio session for Columbia
24 August 1964
Nashville

| — | Wind Me Up (Let Me Go) | A-side |

Musicians: —
Vocals: The Jordanaires

Producer: Billy Sherrill
Engineer: —
Session hours: —

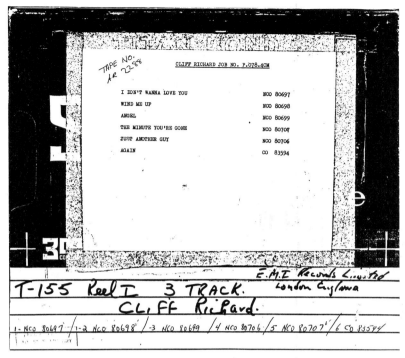

Tape box of recordings made in Nashville and New York. August 1964.

Studio session for Columbia
25 August 1964
Nashville

— The Minute You're Gone   A-side

Musicians: —
Vocals: The Jordanaires

Producer: Billy Sherrill
Engineer: —
Session hours: —

Studio session for Columbia
August 1964
New York

15	Everyone Needs Someone To Love	Love Is Forever
08	Through The Eye Of A Needle	Love Is Forever
—	I Don't Wanna Love You	Cliff Richard
—	Angel	Cliff Richard
—	Just Another Guy	B-side

Acetate for personal use.

Musicians: —
Vocals: —

Producer: —
Engineer: —
Session hours: —

Studio session for Columbia
2/3 October 1964
EMI Lisbon

04	O Mio Signore (The Questions)	When In Rome
04	Come Prima (For The First Time)	When In Rome
04	Concerto D'Automno (Autumn Concerto)	When In Rome
—	Casa Senza Finestre	When In Rome
04	Arrivederci Roma	When In Rome
03	Legata Ad Un Granello Di Sabbia	When In Rome
—	Per Un Bacio D'Amor	When In Rome
05	Che Cosa Del Mia Amore	When In Rome
05	Carina	When In Rome
05	Volare	When In Rome
—	Dicitencello Vuie (Just Say I Love Her)	When In Rome
08	*I Only Know I Love You*	*Unissued*
—	Maria Ninguem (Maria's Her Name)	When In Rome
—	Non L'Ascoltare (Don't Talk To Him)	When In Rome

Guitars: Hank Marvin
   Bruce Welch
Bass: John Rostill
Drums: Brian Bennett
The Norrie Paramor Orchestra

Producers: John Lee / M. Di Ponti
Engineer: —
Session hours: —

Tape box showing foreign language recordings for tape to tape purposes only.

Studio session for Columbia
10 October 1964
Abbey Road

— Nur Mit Dir
(On The Beach)   German
release
— Das Ist Die Frage Aller Fragen
(Spanish Harlem)   German
release

Producer: Norrie Paramor
Engineer: —
Recorded in studio 2
Session hours: 7.00 pm–10.00 pm

Cliff's vocals were overdubbed onto the existing tracks for release in Germany.

Studio session for Columbia
15 October 1964
Abbey Road

05	I'm In Love With You	B-side
03	Evening Comes	Aladdin
07	I Could Easily Fall In Love With You	A-side
—	Havin' Fun	Aladdin

Guitars: Hank Marvin
Bruce Welch
Bass: John Rostill
Drums: Brian Bennett

Producer: Norrie Paramor
Engineers: Malcolm Addy / Ken Scott
Recorded in studio 2
Session hours: 2.30 pm–6.00 pm and
7.00 pm–11.00 pm

Studio session for Columbia
16 October 1964
Abbey Road

04	Widow Twankey Song	Aladdin
04	I'm Feeling Oh So Lonely	Aladdin
11	This Is My Special Day	A-side

The Norrie Paramor Orchestra
The Mike Sammes Singers
Vocals: Una Stubbs / Joan Palethorpe / Audrey Bayley

Producer: Norrie Paramor
Engineers: Malcolm Addy / Ken Scott
Recorded in studio 2
Session hours: 7.00 pm–10.00 pm

Cliff and the Shadows 1966. From left to right: John Rostill, Hank Marvin, Cliff, Bruce Welch and Brian Bennett.

Studio session for Columbia
17 October 1964
Abbey Road

05	There's Gotta Be A Way	Aladdin
04	I've Said Too Many Things	Aladdin
sp	Make Ev'ry Day A Carnival Day	Aladdin

The Norrie Paramor Orchestra
The Mike Sammes Singers

Producer: Norrie Paramor
Engineers: Malcolm Addy / Ken Scott
Recorded in studio 2
Session hours: 7.00 pm–9.30 pm

Make Ev'ry Day A Carnival Day is spliced from takes 5 and 6.

Studio session for Columbia
17 October 1964
Abbey Road

03	Emperor Theme	Aladdin
06	Street Scene	Aladdin
—	Dance Of The Warriors	Aladdin
02	The Dragon Dance	Aladdin
04	Ballet – Part 1	Aladdin
07	Ballet – Part 2	Aladdin
09	Ballet – Part 3	Aladdin
10	Ballet – Part 4	Aladdin

The Norrie Paramor Orchestra

Producer: Norrie Paramor
Engineers: Malcolm Addy / Ken Scott
Recorded in studio 2
Session hours: 2.30 pm–6.00 pm

These are orchestral tracks for the Aladdin LP.

Studio session for Columbia
21 October 1964
Abbey Road

05	Friends	Aladdin

Guitars: Hank Marvin
      Bruce Welch

Bass: John Rostill
Drums: Brian Bennett
The Norrie Paramor Orchestra
The Mike Sammes Singers

Producer: Norrie Paramor
Engineers: Malcolm Addy / Ken Scott
Recorded in studio 3
Session hours: 2.30 pm–3.30 pm

Studio session for Columbia
4 April 1965
Abbey Road

—	Whatcha' Gonna Do About It	—
—	Just A Little Bit Too Late	B-side

Guitars: Hank Marvin
      Bruce Welch
Bass: John Rostill
Drums: Brian Bennett

Producer: Norrie Paramor
Engineer: —
Recorded in studio 2
Session hours: 2.30 pm–5.30 pm

Studio session for Columbia
14 April 1965
Abbey Road

—	Boom Boom	Take Four EP

Producer: Norrie Paramor
Engineer: —
Recorded in studio: —
Session hours: —

Studio session for Columbia
15 April 1965
Abbey Road

—	Es War Keine So Wunderbar Wie Du (I Could Easily Fall In Love)	German release
—	Es Könnte Schon Morgen Sein (The Minute You're Gone)	German release

| — | *It Could Already Be Tomorrow* | *Unissued* |
| — | *As Wonderful As You* | *Unissued* |

Producer: Norrie Paramor
Engineer: —
Recorded in studio 3
Session hours: 7.00 pm–10.00 pm

Cliff's vocals dubbed onto existing tracks for release in Germany.

Studio session for Columbia
10 May 1965
Abbey Road

—	Someday (You'll Want Me To Love You)	Love Is Forever
—	Have I Told You Lately That I Love You	Love Is Forever
—	Look Before You Love	B-side
—	*Deep Purple*	*Unissued*
—	The Time In Between	A-side
—	Into Each Life Some Rain Must Fall	Finders Keepers

Guitars: Hank Marvin
        Bruce Welch
Bass: John Rostill
Drums: Brian Bennett

Acetate of unissued song 1965.

Producer: Norrie Paramor
Engineer: —
Recorded in studio 1
Session hours: 2.30 pm–5.30 pm and 7.00 pm–10.00 pm

Studio session for Columbia
10 June 1965
Abbey Road

—	Long Ago	Love Is Forever
—	I'll Walk Alone	Love Is Forever
—	A Summer Place	Love Is Forever
—	My Foolish Heart	Love Is Forever

The Norrie Paramor Orchestra

Producer: Norrie Paramor
Engineer: —
Recorded in studio 2
Session hours: 7.00 pm–10.00 pm

Studio session for Columbia
4 October 1965
Abbey Road

06	The Girl From Ipanema	Kinda Latin
03	Quiet Nights Of Quiet Stars	Kinda Latin
04	Our Day Will Come	Kinda Latin
01	Meditation	Kinda Latin

The Bernard Ebbinghouse Orchestra

Producer: Norrie Paramor
Engineer: Peter Bown
Recorded in studio 2
Session hours: 7.00 pm–9.30 pm

Studio session for Columbia
5 October 1965
Abbey Road

| — | The Night | B-side |

Producer: Norrie Paramor
Engineer: Peter Bown
Recorded in studio 2
Session hours: —

Studio session for Columbia
7 October 1965
Abbey Road

03	Quando, Quando, Quando	Kinda Latin
03	Eso Beso	Kinda Latin
06	Fly Me To The Moon	Kinda Latin
03	Blame It On The Bossa Nova	Kinda Latin

The Reg Guest Orchestra

Producer: Norrie Paramor
Engineer: Peter Bown
Recorded in studio 2
Session hours: 7.00 pm–10.15 pm

Studio session for Columbia
22 October 1965
Abbey Road

07	Concrete And Clay	Kinda Latin
09	Blowin' In The Wind	Kinda Latin
04	One Note Samba	Kinda Latin
06	Come Closer To Me	Kinda Latin

The Les Reed Orchestra

Producer: Norrie Paramor
Engineer: Peter Bown
Recorded in studio 3
Session hours: 2.30 pm–6.00 pm

Studio session for Columbia
27 October 1965
Abbey Road

—	Glaub Nur Mir (On My Word)	German release
—	Nur Bei Dir Bin Ich Zu Haus (Wind Me Up)	German release

Producer: —
Engineer: —
Recorded in studio 2
Session hours: 7.00 pm–10.00 pm

Superimposition of German lyrics onto German backing tracks.

Studio session for Columbia
17 November 1965
Abbey Road

—	*I Love You The Way You Are*	*Unissued*
—	*I Still Send Her Flowers*	*Unissued*
—	Close to Cathy	Two A Penny
—	Visions	A-side

The Bernard Ebbinghouse Orchestra
The Mike Sammes Singers

Producer: Norrie Paramor
Engineer: —
Recorded in studio 2
Session hours: 7.00 pm–10.55 pm

Studio session for Columbia
18 November 1965
Abbey Road

04	*Sooner Or Later*	*Unissued*
07	*A Spoonful Of Sugar*	*Unissued*
04	*Zip-A-Dee-Doo-Dah*	*Unissued*
05	*Chim Chim Cheree*	*Unissued*

Orchestra: —

Producer: Norrie Paramor
Engineer: Malcolm Addy
Recorded in studio 2
Session hours: 7.00 pm–10.30 pm

5

Don't Stop Me Now

1966–1967

───────────────────── **The Records** ─────────────────────

Blue Turns To Grey / Somebody Loses	Single	15 / —
Visions / What Would I Do	Single	7 / —
Time Drags By / La La La Song	Single	10 / —
In The Country / Finders Keepers	Single	6 / —
It's All Over / Why Wasn't I Born Rich	Single	9 / —
I'll Come Running / I Get The Feeling	Single	26 / —
The Day I Met Marie / Our Storybook	Single	10 / —
All My Love / Sweet Little Jesus Boy	Single	6 / —
Wind Me Up	EP	
Hits From 'When In Rome'	EP	
Love Is Forever	EP	
Thunderbirds Are Go	EP	
La La La La La	EP	
Cinderella	EP	
Carol Singers	EP	

EP chart positions taken from 'Record Retailer'

Kinda Latin	LP	9
Finders Keepers	LP	6
Cinderella	LP	30
Don't Stop Me Now	LP	23
Good News	LP	37

All the singles that were released in 1966 became top twenty hits. *In The Country* taken from the CINDERELLA cast album was the one with the most impressive chart placing, but somehow the momentum was not maintained by the album. Given the quality of the previous single *Time Drags By* from the FINDERS KEEPERS soundtrack it seems incredible that it did not reach higher than the number 10 spot. Of the four singles released the following year, no fewer than three reached the top ten. The single that did not do so well – *I'll Come Running* – failed to reach the top twenty, stalling at number 26.

Two of the five albums released in this period did well and reached the top ten of the album charts. KINDA LATIN featured latin flavoured material with songs like *Blame It On The Bossa Nova*, *The Girl From Ipanema* and *One Note Samba*, a far cry not only from rock 'n' roll, but also from pop music as it was developing at that time. But the album sold well enough to reach number 9. The follow-up album, the soundtrack of the film FINDERS KEEPERS, was even stronger than KINDA LATIN, and had a top ten single to spur interest. The album outdid all the others of this period by reaching the number 6 spot and staying on the chart for 18 weeks. DON'T STOP ME NOW was released next, but as there was no hit single to boost sales the album suffered chartwise whereas it could have been a smash album with its combination of some contemporary hits of the time and some rock 'n' roll standards. Sales of Cliff's first sacred album GOOD NEWS were not impressive, but considering the limited market for this kind of music the figures were still impressive enough.

The same trend was reflected in the sales of the CAROL SINGERS EP that featured Cliff singing carols a cappella with a group of music

Publicity shot from 1967.

teachers. None of the EPs released in this period notched up enough sales to make it to the EP or singles charts, even though some of the material on some of the EPs appeared only in that format.

The Sessions

Finders Keepers soundtrack sessions:
    Abbey Road
Studio sessions for Columbia: Abbey Road
Cinderella cast sessions: Abbey Road
Two A Penny soundtrack sessions: Abbey Road
Live recordings for Columbia: Tokyo

Of the material selected for the April soundtrack session, *Time Drags By* stands out as the one to take advantage of the multi-track system to good effect. For this, a basic track was laid down after which Cliff and the Shadows double-tracked their vocals eventually resulting in eight vocals on the record, which surprisingly did not become a major hit but still showed conclusively that Cliff was still a force to be reckoned with and could make records that were artistically significant. Work continued on FINDERS KEEPERS through to September with the Shadows providing musical and vocal backing joined by the Bernard Ebbinghouse Orchestra.

In October, a variety of material was taped for the DON'T STOP ME NOW album, the LA LA LA LA LA EP, and two well crafted pop songs for single release. The Bernard Ebbinghouse Orchestra was invited to provide musical accompaniment again as a result of their outstanding work on the previous sessions.

As had happened before with the ALADDIN pantomime at the London Palladium, CINDERELLA necessitated soundtrack sessions with all the material for the album being recorded through to November with, of course, the Shadows providing the score and musical accompaniment, and the Mike Sammes Singers adding some excellent vocal back-ups. Jackie Lee duetted with Cliff on *Wouldn't It Be Nice* taped at one of the November sessions.

The January/February sessions provided the remainder of the material needed to fill out the DON'T STOP ME NOW album. Some breathtaking rock performances were taped with musical backing from the Mike Leander Orchestra. *Good Golly Miss Molly*, *My Babe* and *Move It* were the gems.

The sessions in April and May were Cliff's first excursion into the gospel field, and provided all the tracks for the GOOD NEWS album. Sacred music had become very much a part of Cliff's life in the wake of his Christian conviction, so it was only natural for him to record this type of material.

After the July session that provided a number of songs for the TWO A PENNY soundtrack, Cliff did not enter the studio again until September when work was geared towards producing a Christmas EP. The tracks for CAROL SINGERS were done without any musical backing or orchestral arrangements, and were performed a cappella with the Mastersingers, a Christian group of music teachers.

For the last recordings of the year, and to have enough material for an album, Columbia simply recorded one of Cliff's live dates in Japan, and although there was some reshuffling as far as the Cliff classics went, the inclusion of some newer songs did not really offer anything new from a musical point of view. However, CLIFF IN JAPAN became a worldwide top seller appealing to the international audience the album was aimed at. *Bachelor Boy* and *It's All In The Game* were two extra tracks released only on the Japanese issue of the album.

Studio session for Columbia
17 January 1966
Abbey Road

| — | Blue Turns To Grey | A-side |
| — | Somebody Loses | B-side |

Guitars: Hank Marvin
        Bruce Welch
Bass: John Rostill
Drums: Brian Bennett

Cliff and Hank rehearsing during session.

Producer: Norrie Paramor
Engineer: —
Recorded in studio 2
Session hours: 7.00 pm–11.15 pm

**Film soundtrack recordings for
Finders Keepers
26 April 1966
Abbey Road**

10	Oh Señorita	Finders Keepers
01	Finders Keepers	Finders Keepers
04	Time Drags By	A-side

Guitars: Hank Marvin
        Bruce Welch
Bass: John Rostill
Drums: Brian Bennett

Producer: Norrie Paramor
Engineers: Malcolm Addy / Peter Vince / Richard Langham
Recorded in studio 2
Session hours: 2.30 pm–5.30 pm and 7.00 pm–12.30 am

**Film soundtrack recordings for
Finders Keepers
27 April 1966
Abbey Road**

06	*This Day*	*Unissued*

Guitars: Hank Marvin
        Bruce Welch
Bass: John Rostill
Drums: Brian Bennett

Producer: Norrie Paramor
Engineers: Peter Vince / Richard Langham
Recorded in studio 2
Session hours: 7.00 pm–2.00 am

**Film soundtrack recordings for
Finders Keepers
28 April 1966
Abbey Road**

02	Washerwoman	Finders Keepers
04	*Oh Señorita*	*Unissued*
01	La La La Song	B-side

Guitars: Hank Marvin
        Bruce Welch
Bass: John Rostill
Drums: Brian Bennett

Producer: Norrie Paramor
Engineers: Peter Vince / Richard Langham
Recorded in studio 3
Session hours: 2.30 pm–6.00 pm and 7.00 pm–midnight

Oh Señorita is the film version.

**Studio session for Columbia
5 May 1966
Studio Unknown**

—	Shooting Star	Thunderbirds Are Go EP

Guitars: Hank Marvin
        Bruce Welch
Bass: John Rostill
Drums: Brian Bennett

Producer: —
Engineer: —
Session hours: —

**Studio session for Columbia
13 May 1966
Abbey Road**

—	Yours	German release
—	Was Ist Dabei (The Time In Between)	German release

Producer: Norrie Paramor
Engineer: —
Recorded in studio 3
Session hours: 7.00 pm–10.00 pm

Superimposition of German lyrics onto original backing tracks.

**Studio session for Columbia
22 May 1966
Abbey Road**

—	What Would I Do For The Love Of A Girl	B-side

Guitars: Hank Marvin
       Bruce Welch
Bass: John Rostill
Drums: Brian Bennett

Producers: David Paramor / Norrie Paramor
Engineer: —
Recorded in studio 3
Session hours: 7.00 pm–10.00 pm

**Film soundtrack recordings for
Finders Keepers
4 June 1966
Abbey Road**

—	This Day	Finders Keepers

Guitars: Hank Marvin
       Bruce Welch
Bass: John Rostill
Drums: Brian Bennett

Producer: Norrie Paramor
Engineer: —
Recorded in studio 3
Session hours: 7.00 pm–10.00 pm

**Studio session for Columbia
19 September 1966
Abbey Road**

—	*Solitary Man*	*Unissued*
15	*You Gotta Tell Me*	*Unissued*

03	I'll Be Back	Don't Stop Me Now
—	*Things We Said Today*	*Unissued*

The Bernard Ebbinghouse Orchestra

Producer: Norrie Paramor
Engineers: Peter Vince / Richard Langham
Recorded in studio 2
Session hours: 7.00 pm–10.00 pm

**Studio session for Columbia
20 September 1966
Abbey Road**

—	Time	Sincerely Cliff
03	Run To The Door	Finders Keepers
07	*It's All Over*	*Unissued*
02	Where Did The Summer Go	Finders Keepers

The Bernard Ebbinghouse Orchestra
The Mike Sammes Singers

Producer: Norrie Paramor
Engineers: Peter Vince / Richard Langham
Recorded in studio 2
Session hours: 7.00 pm–10.00 pm

**Studio session for Columbia
21 September 1966
Abbey Road**

05	Never Knew What Love Could Do	La La La La La EP
02	*La La La La La*	*Unissued*
03	*One Fine Day*	*Unissued*
06	I Saw Her Standing There	Don't Stop Me Now

Orchestra: —

Producer: Norrie Paramor
Engineers: Peter Vince / Richard Langham
Recorded in studio 2
Session hours: 7.00 pm–10.15 pm

Studio session for Columbia
11 October 1966
Abbey Road

—	One Fine Day	Don't Stop Me Now
—	You Gotta Tell Me	Don't Stop Me Now
—	Things We Said Today	La La La La La EP
—	It's All Over	A-side
—	La La La La La	La La La La La EP
—	Solitary Man	La La La La La EP

The Bernard Ebbinghouse Orchestra

Producer: Norrie Paramor
Engineer: Peter Vince
Recorded in studio 2
Session hours: —

Studio session for Columbia
14 October 1966
Abbey Road

06	*Why Wasn't I Born Rich*	*Unissued*
06	Come Sunday	Cinderella
05	*Hey Doctor Man*	*Unissued*

Guitars: Hank Marvin
        Bruce Welch
Bass: John Rostill
Drums: Brian Bennett

Producer: Norrie Paramor
Engineers: Peter Vince / Richard Langham
Recorded in studio 2
Session hours: 2.30 pm–6.00 pm and
7.00 pm–12.15 am

Studio session for Columbia
17 October 1966
Abbey Road

08	She Needs Him More Than Me	Cinderella
05	*Somewhere*	*Unissued*

Guitars: Hank Marvin
        Bruce Welch
Bass: John Rostill
Drums: Brian Bennett

Producer: Norrie Paramor
Engineers: Peter Vince / Richard Langham
Recorded in studio 2
Session hours: 7.00 pm–11.30 pm

Studio session for Columbia
19 October 1966
Abbey Road

sp	Homeward Bound	Don't Stop Me Now
05	Don't	Don't Stop Me Now
02	Save The Last Dance For Me	Don't Stop Me Now
01	Dizzy Miss Lizzy	Don't Stop Me Now

Orchestra: —
Vocals: The Breakaways

Producers: Norrie Paramor / David Paramor
Engineers: Peter Vince / Richard Langham
Recorded in studio 2
Session hours: 7.00 pm–10.15 pm

Homeward Bound is an edit of takes 1 and 7.

Studio session for Columbia
9 November 1966
Abbey Road

02	The King's Place	Cinderella
05	*Peace And Quiet*	*Unissued*
—	Poverty	Cinderella

Guitars: Hank Marvin
        Bruce Welch
Bass: John Rostill
Drums: Brian Bennett
Vocals: The Mike Sammes Singers

Producer: Norrie Paramor
Engineers: Peter Vince / Richard Langham
Recorded in studio 2
Session hours: 2.30 pm–5.30 pm

Studio session for Columbia
10 November 1966
Abbey Road

| — | Das Glück Ist Rosarot | German release |

Producer: Norrie Paramor
Engineer: —
Recorded in studio 2
Session hours: 7.00 pm–10.00 pm

German lyrics overdubbed onto the existing tracks for German release.

Studio session for Columbia
11 November 1966
Abbey Road

08	The Hunt	Cinderella
07	Wouldn't It Be Nice (If Our Dreams Came True)	Cinderella
05	Dare I Love Him	Cinderella
—	*In The Country*	*Unissued*

The Norrie Paramor Orchestra
Vocals: The Mike Sammes Singers

Duet on Wouldn't It Be Nice: Jackie Lee.

Producer: Norrie Paramor
Engineers: Peter Vince / Richard Langham
Recorded in studio 2
Session hours: 2.30 pm–5.30 pm

Studio session for Columbia
16 November 1966
Abbey Road

06	Hey Doctor Man	Cinderella
04	In The Country	A-side
05	Peace And Quiet	Cinderella
—	Welcome To Stoneybroke	Cinderella

Guitars: Hank Marvin
        Bruce Welch
Bass: John Rostill
Drums: Brian Bennett

Producer: Norrie Paramor
Engineers: Peter Vince / Richard Langham
Recorded in studio 3
Session hours: 7.00 pm–midnight

Studio session for Columbia
19 November 1966
Abbey Road

—	*Peace And Quiet*	*Unissued*
—	Why Wasn't I Born Rich	Cinderella

The Norrie Paramor Orchestra
Vocals: The Mike Sammes Singers

Producer: Norrie Paramor
Engineer: —
Recorded in studio 2
Session hours: 2.30 pm–5.30 pm

Studio session for Columbia
15 January 1967
Abbey Road

04	Baby It's You	Don't Stop Me Now
03	Don't Make Promises	Don't Stop Me Now
04	Hang On To A Dream	Don't Stop Me Now
04	Heartbeat	Don't Stop Me Now

Orchestra: —

Producer: Norrie Paramor
Engineers: Peter Vince / Richard Langham
Recorded in studio 2
Session hours: 7.00 pm–10.00 pm

Studio session for Columbia
5 February 1967
Abbey Road

08	Shout	Don't Stop Me Now
03	My Babe	Don't Stop Me Now

06	Good Golly Miss Molly	Don't Stop Me Now
54	Move It	Don't Stop Me Now

Orchestra: —

Producer: Norrie Paramor
Engineers: Peter Vince / Richard Langham
Recorded in studio 2
Session hours: 7.00 pm–10.15 pm

Studio session for Columbia
24 April 1967
Abbey Road

—	I'll Come Running	A-side
—	I Get The Feeling	B-side
—	I'll Make It All Up To You	Tracks 'n' Grooves
—	Our Storybook	B-side

Orchestra: —

Producer: Norrie Paramor
Engineer: —
Recorded in studio: —
Session hours: —

Studio session for Columbia
25 April 1967
Abbey Road

—	Bilder Von Dir (Visions)	German A-side

Producer: —
Engineer: —
Recorded in studio 2
Session hours: —

Studio session for Columbia
27 April 1967
Abbey Road

02	We Shall Be Changed	Good News
05	Mary What You Gonna Call That Pretty Little Baby King	Good News
03	Get On Board Little Children	Good News
03	Go Where I Send Thee	Good News

Guitars: Hank Marvin
         Bruce Welch
Bass: John Rostill
Drums: Brian Bennett
Vocals: —

Producer: Norrie Paramor
Engineer: Peter Vince
Recorded in studio 2
Session hours: 7.00 pm–11.00 pm

Studio session for Columbia
28 April 1967
Abbey Road

03	*All In The April Evening*	*Unissued*
02	Sweet Little Jesus Boy	B-side
03	*Were You There*	*Unissued*
02	What A Friend We Have In Jesus	Good News
04	When I Survey The Wondrous Cross	Good News

The Norrie Paramor Orchestra
Soprano voice: Pat Clark

Producer: Norrie Paramor
Engineer: Peter Vince
Recorded in studio 2
Session hours: 7.00 pm–10.00 pm

Studio session for Columbia
3 May 1967
Abbey Road

04	Take My Hand, Precious Lord	Good News
06	Just A Closer Walk With Thee	Good News
02	*Star Of Hope*	*Unissued*
sp	It Is No Secret	Good News
sp	May The Good Lord Bless And Keep You	Good News

The Bernard Ebbinghouse Orchestra

Producer: Norrie Paramor
Engineer: Peter Vince
Recorded in studio 2
Session hours: 7.00 pm–10.30 pm

It Is No Secret is an edit of takes 1 and 5.

May The Good Lord is an edit of takes 1 and 3.

Studio session for Columbia
4 May 1967
Abbey Road

06	23rd Psalm	Good News
04	The King Of Love My Shepherd Is	Good News
04	*There Is A Green Hill Far Away*	*Unissued*
03	*Praise My Soul The King Of Heaven*	*Unissued*
02	All Glory Laud And Honour	Good News

The Norrie Paramor Orchestra

Producer: Norrie Paramor
Engineer: Peter Vince
Recorded in studio 2
Session hours: 7.00 pm–10.15 pm

Studio session for Columbia
13 May 1967
Abbey Road

—	Good News	Good News
—	*Words*	*Unissued*

The Norrie Paramor Orchestra

Producer: Norrie Paramor
Engineer: Peter Vince
Recorded in studio 2
Session hours: 7.00 pm–10.00 pm

Studio session for Columbia
1 June 1967
Abbey Road

—	The Day I Met Marie	A-side
—	Red Rubber Ball	Two A Penny
—	Put My Mind At Ease	Tracks 'n' Grooves
—	I'd Just Be Fool Enough	Tracks 'n' Grooves

Mike Leander Orchestra

Producer: Norrie Paramor
Engineer: —
Recorded in studio: —
Session hours: —

Film soundtrack recordings for Two A Penny
1 July 1967
Abbey Road

—	Two A Penny	Two A Penny
—	I'll Love You Forever Today	A-side
—	Twist And Shout	Two A Penny
—	Questions, Questions	Two A Penny

Mike Leander Orchestra

Producer: Norrie Paramor
Engineer: —
Recorded in studio 2
Session hours: 2.30 pm–5.30 pm

Studio session for Columbia
10 September 1967
Abbey Road

—	*It Came Upon A Midnight Clear*	*Unissued*
—	In The Bleak Mid-Winter	Carol Singers EP
—	God Rest Ye Merry Gentlemen	Carol Singers EP
—	While Shepherds Watched	Carol Singers EP
—	Little Town Of Bethlehem	Carol Singers EP
—	*Twelve Days Of Christmas*	*Unissued*
—	Unto Us A Boy Is Born	Carol Singers EP
08	*The Holly And The Ivy*	*Unissued*

Vocals: The Mastersingers

Producer: Norrie Paramor
Engineer: Peter Vince
Recorded in studio 2
Session hours: 2.30 pm–5.30 pm and 7.00 pm–10.45 pm

MONO/STEREO 4 TRACK   **RECORDING SHEET**   Date of Session 4ᵀᴴ May '67   Job No : 35,080

Sheet : 1 of : 1   Class : POPULAR   Overall Title _____

	ARTISTIC INFORMATION						COSTING INFORMATION						
ARTISTE(S) AND/OR CAST	CLIFF RICHARD		CONDUCTOR	MR NORRIE PARAMOR			MATERIALS USED	3 × 8"		ORDER NUMBER			
			ORCHESTRA				SESSION BOOKED TIME	7.00 — 10.00		COMPANY		COLUMBIA	
			ACCOMPANIMENT				SESSION ACTUAL	7.00 — 10.15		STUDIO/CONTROL ROOM		2 / 2	
			ART. DEPT. REP.	MR NORRIE PARAMOR			SET-UP/PLAYBACK	½ / 1¼		ENGINEERS		PRV/MAS.	
TITLES and Matrix Nos.	AUTHOR/COMPOSER/ PUBLISHER		REEL NUMBERS	*ALSE STARTS	TAKE No.	TAKE DETAILS FROM — TO		DUR.	M	REMARKS			
23ᴿᴰ PSALM	*A & B		E 64232	1	2	COMPLETE		2.35					
	J. IRVINE		4 TRACK		3	B.D.							
	ARR. N. PARAMOR			4, 5	6	COMPLETE		2.31	BEST				
THE KING MY LOVE A SHEPHERD IS	*A & B				1	COMPLETE		2.41					
	TRAD. ARR. N. PARAMOR			2, 3	4	COMPLETE		2.37	BEST				
THERE IS A GREEN HILL FAR AWAY	*A & B		E 64233	1	2	COMPLETE		2.13		} EDIT FOR INTRO			
	HORSLEY		4 TRACK		3	COMPLETE		2.15					
	ARR. N. PARAMOR				4	COMPLETE		2.15	BEST				
PRAISE MY SOUL THE KING OF HEAVEN	*A & B				2	COMPLETE		2.39					
	GOSS				3	COMPLETE		2.41	BEST				
	ARR. N. PARAMOR												
ALL GLORY LAND AND HONOUR	*A & B		E 64234	1	2	COMPLETE		3.32	BEST				
	TRAD. ARR. N. PARAMOR		4 TRACK										

Ref. 9864

**Studio session for Columbia
27 September 1967
Abbey Road**

—	I'll Come Running	German release
—	The Day I Met Marie	German release
—	The Day I Met Marie	Italian release
—	I Got The Feeling	German release

The Bernard Ebbinghouse Orchestra

Producer: Norrie Paramor
Engineer: —
Recorded in studio 2
Session hours: 7.00 pm–10.30 pm

Some of the above titles are backing tracks only.

**Studio session for Columbia
28 September 1967
Abbey Road**

—	Es Ist Nicht Gut, Allein Zu Sein	German release
—	Mrs Emily Jones	German release
—	I'll Come Running	German release
—	The Day I Met Marie	Italian release
—	I Got The Feeling	Italian release

Producer: Norrie Paramor
Engineer: —
Recorded in studio 2
Session hours: 7.00 pm–11.15 pm

These titles are vocal overdubs of previously recorded backing tracks.

**Studio session for Columbia
5 October 1967
Abbey Road**

—	All My Love	A-side
—	Don't Ask Me To Be Friends	Tracks 'n' Grooves
—	*I Only Live To Love You*	*Unissued*

The Bernard Ebbinghouse Orchestra
Vocals: The Mike Sammes Singers

Producer: Norrie Paramor
Engineer: —
Recorded in studio 2
Session hours: 7.00 pm–10.15 pm

**Studio session for Columbia
11 October 1967
Abbey Road**

—	Cloudy	Two A Penny
—	*The Letter*	*Unissued*
—	The Girl Can't Help It	Tracks 'n' Grooves
—	For Emily Wherever I May Find Her	Sincerely Cliff

Mike Leander Orchestra
Vocals: —

Producer: Norrie Paramor
Engineer: —
Recorded in studio 2
Session hours: 7.00 pm–10.00 pm

**Live recordings for Columbia
18 October 1967
Shibuya Public Hall, Tokyo, Japan**

—	*In The Country*	*Unissued*
—	Dynamite	Cliff In Japan
—	*Bachelor Boy*	*Unissued*
—	Finders Keepers	Cliff In Japan
—	On The Beach	Cliff In Japan

— Evergreen Tree   Cliff In Japan

— Visions   Cliff In Japan

— What'd I Say   Cliff In Japan

— Shout   Cliff In Japan

— Twist And Shout   Cliff In Japan

— *Angel*   *Unissued*

— *It's All In The Game*   *Unissued*

— The Minute You're Gone   Cliff In Japan

— *The Day I Met Marie*   *Unissued*

— I'll Come Running   Cliff In Japan

— *The Next Time*   *Unissued*

— Spanish Harlem   Cliff In Japan

— Move It   Cliff In Japan

— *Dizzy Miss Lizzy*   *Unissued*

— Hang On To A Dream   Cliff In Japan

— *Good Golly, Miss Molly*   *Unissued*

— La La La La La   Cliff In Japan

— Living Doll   Cliff In Japan

— Medley: Let's Make A Memory   Cliff In Japan

— The Young Ones   Cliff In Japan

— Lucky Lips   Cliff In Japan

— Summer Holiday   Cliff In Japan

— We Say Yeah   Cliff In Japan

The Norrie Paramor Orchestra

Producer: Norrie Paramor
Engineer: —
Session hours: —

6

Tracks 'n' Grooves

1968–1970

---- **The Records** ----

Congratulations / High 'n' Dry	Single	1/—	
I'll Love You Forever Today /			
Girl You'll Be A Woman Soon	Single	27/—	
Marianne / Mr Nice	Single	22/—	
Don't Forget To Catch Me /			
What's More I Don't Need Her	Single	21/—	
Good Times / Occasional Rain	Single	12/—	
Big Ship / She's Leaving You	Single	8/—	
Throw Down A Line / Reflections	Single	7/—	
With The Eyes Of A Child /			
So Long	Single	20/—	
The Joy Of Living / Boogatoo /			
Leave My Woman Alone	Single	25/—	
Goodbye Sam, Hello Samantha /			
You Never Can Tell	Single	6/—	
I Ain't Got Time Anymore /			
Monday Comes Too Soon	Single	21/—	

Congratulations	EP

EP chart positions taken from 'Record Retailer'

Cliff In Japan	LP	29
Two A Penny	LP	
Established 1958	LP	30
The Best of Cliff	LP	5
Sincerely Cliff	LP	24
It'll Be Me	LP	
Cliff 'Live At The Talk Of The		
Town'	LP	
All My Love	LP	
About That Man	LP	
Tracks 'n' Grooves	LP	37
His Land	LP	

The Bill Martin and Phil Coulter composition *Congratulations* was selected as the winning UK entry for the Eurovision Song Contest, and became Cliff's first number 1 single since *The Minute You're Gone* had hit the top of the charts in 1965. Another three singles were released in 1968 but a slump in sales was illustrated by the fact that none of them reached the top twenty. However, all the singles released the following year brought Cliff back into that top twenty. *Big Ship* packed enough commercial appeal to reach the number 8 spot, and *Throw Down A Line* credited to Cliff *and* Hank eventually peaked at number 7. Somehow, 1970 turned out to be a mediocre year, although *Goodbye Sam, Hello Samantha* was one of the more successful recordings and consequently

reached higher on the charts than the other two singles released that year.

Sales of the albums released during this period followed the same mediocre pattern as the 1970 singles with a noticeable decline in chart placings, though the picture was definitely better as far as the new 'hits' compilation was concerned. THE BEST OF CLIFF was the only one to reach the top five of the album chart. None of the other albums reached any higher than number 24, despite the fact that one of three budget priced albums featured new 'live'

recordings of Cliff's 1968 shows at London's Talk Of The Town. The full price albums didn't stir up much chart action either. After ESTABLISHED 1958, a tenth anniversary set that shared half the album with the Shadows, a pair of religious albums ABOUT THAT MAN and HIS LAND simply went unnoticed. The fact that Cliff's final EP CONGRATULATIONS did not make the charts reflects a change in consumer habits. By this time budget price album sales had completely overtaken the sale of EPs.

The Sessions

Studio sessions for EMI: Abbey Road
Live recordings for EMI: Talk Of The Town,
   London
Studio sessions for EMI: Chappell Studios
Studio session for EMI: IBC Studios
Studio session for EMI: Advision

During the February 1968 sessions, Cliff recorded all six prospective UK entries for the Eurovision Song Contest in preparation for their televising. Of these *Congratulations* was chosen as the favourite and became the hit single of this period. The track was later re-recorded in no fewer than four foreign language versions at the April sessions.

For some reason the session on May 29 never really got off the ground, although it seems probable the session was set up to provide material suitable for the tenth anniversary album ESTABLISHED 1958. However that may be, the thread of the session was only taken up again in June and July when Cliff completed the tracks for his half of the album – a new batch of Shadows recordings made up the other half.

The live recordings taped during this period were taken from the three shows recorded at London's Talk Of The Town between 30 May and 1 June. For the repertoire the basic formula of a mixture of old hits and covers was maintained. As far as the covers went, Cliff included a rousing rendition of *Shout* which had been a top ten hit for Lulu; a knockout version of *Ain't Nothing But A Houseparty* and a number of others. Once more the Norrie Paramor Orchestra provided the musical

accompaniment and arrangements, while the Breakaways were called on for vocal backing on most of the songs. For some reason these recordings were considered only suitable for release in the shape of a budget price album retailing at under £1.

The songs Cliff was to record next would be German language versions of many of his major hit singles and some of the more obscure album tracks. There was also a handful of songs never recorded in English.

For the Tyne Tees Television network series "Life With Johnny" both the instrumental backing and vocals by Cliff and the Settlers were pre-recorded at the sessions over December 1968 to January 1969. The 22 songs taped were all featured in the six programmes of modern parables designed for religious broadcasting. The original plan to release a selection of these recordings as a soundtrack album was dropped along the way. It may well be that EMI felt its release might have had a limited appeal from a commercial point of view.

Besides the sessions aimed at producing new singles and album tracks for SINCERELY CLIFF and TRACKS 'N' GROOVES, a variety of religious material was recorded. One single session in February 1970 provided all the items for ABOUT THAT MAN – a combination of songs and readings from the New Testament. However, there is no information filed relating to recording dates or studio locations for HIS LAND – the soundtrack for a film Cliff made for the Billy Graham Organisation during a visit to Israel.

**Studio session for Columbia
2 February 1968
Abbey Road**

—	Wonderful World	Congratulations EP
—	High 'n' Dry	B-side
—	Do You Remember	Congratulations EP

The Bernard Ebbinghouse Orchestra
The Norrie Paramor Orchestra
Bass guitar: John Paul Jones
      (7.00 pm–9.00 pm only)
Vocals: The Mike Sammes Singers
      (8.00 pm–10.00 pm only)
      Hank Marvin and Bruce Welch
      (8.00 pm–10.00 pm only)

Producer: Norrie Paramor
Engineer: Peter Vince
Recorded in studio 2
Session hours: 7.00 pm–10.30 pm

**Studio session for Columbia
3 February 1968
Abbey Road**

—	The Sound Of The Candyman's Trumpet	Congratulations EP
—	*Shoom Llamma Boom Boom*	*Unissued*
—	Congratulations	A-side

The Norrie Paramor Orchestra
Bass guitar: John Paul Jones
Vocals: The Breakaways

Producer: Norrie Paramor
Engineer: Peter Vince
Recorded in studio 2
Session hours: 8.00 pm–11.30 pm

**Studio session for Columbia
11 February 1968
Abbey Road**

—	Little Rag Doll	Congratulations EP

—	Punch And Judy	Sincerely Cliff
—	Girl You'll Be A Woman Soon	B-side

Mike Leander Orchestra

Producer: Norrie Paramor
Engineer: Peter Vince
Recorded in studio 2
Session hours: 7.00 pm–10.30 pm

**Film soundtrack recordings for
Two A Penny
8 March 1968
Abbey Road**

—	Rattler	Two A Penny
—	Wake Up, Wake Up	Two A Penny
—	The Dreams I Dream	Established 1958
—	Lonely Girl	Two A Penny
—	(And Me) I'm On The Outside Now	Two A Penny
—	What's More I Don't Need Her	B-side
—	London's Not Too Far	Sincerely Cliff

Guitars: Hank Marvin
      Bruce Welch
Bass: John Rostill
Drums: Brian Bennett
Vocals: The Breakaways
Mike Leander Orchestra
(on Two A Penny tracks only)

Producer: Norrie Paramor
Engineer: Peter Vince
Recorded in studio 2
Session hours: 2.30 pm–5.30 pm and
7.00 pm–10.00 pm

Studio session for Columbia
15 March 1968
Abbey Road

—	Sternengold (All My Love)	German release
—	London Ist Nicht Weit (London's Not Too Far)	German release

Mike Leander Orchestra

Producer: Norrie Paramor
Engineer: Peter Vince
Recorded in studio 2
Session hours: 7.00 pm–10.00 pm

Studio session for Columbia
9 April 1968
Abbey Road

—	Man Gratuliert Mir (Congratulations)	German A-side

Orchestra: —

Producer: Norrie Paramor
Engineer: Peter Vince
Recorded in studio 2
Session hours: 7.30 pm–9.45 pm

Studio session for Columbia
23 April 1968
Abbey Road

—	Que Buena Suerte (Congratulations)	Spanish A-side
—	Quelle Histoire Je Suis Millionaire (Congratulations)	French A-side

Producer: Norrie Paramor
Engineer: Peter Vince
Recorded in studio 1
Session hours: 7.00 pm–10.00 pm

The 9 April orchestral track was used for this session.

Studio session for Columbia
3 May 1968
Abbey Road

—	Il Mondo Et Tondo (Congratulations)	Italian A-side

Producer: Norrie Paramor
Engineer: Peter Vince
Recorded in studio 2
Session hours: 7.00 pm–9.15 pm

The 9 April orchestral track was used on this session.

Studio session for Columbia
29 May 1968
Abbey Road

03	Girl On The Bus	Established 1958
01	*Don't Forget To Catch Me*	*Unissued*
01	*What's Behind The Eyes Of Mary*	*Unissued*

Guitars: Hank Marvin
           Bruce Welch
Bass: John Rostill
Drums: Brian Bennett

Producer: Norrie Paramor
Engineer: Peter Vince
Recorded in studio 2
Session hours: 2.30 pm–5.00 pm and
7.00 pm–10.00 pm

Live recordings for Columbia
30 May 1968
Talk Of The Town, London

—	Congratulations – Play On	Live At The Talk Of The Town
—	Shout	Live At The Talk Of The Town
—	All My Love	Live At The Talk Of The Town

—	Ain't Nothing But A Houseparty	Live At The Talk Of The Town
—	Something Good	Live At The Talk Of The Town
—	If Ever I Would Leave You	Live At The Talk Of The Town
—	Girl You'll Be A Woman Soon	Live At The Talk Of The Town
—	London's Not Too Far	Live At The Talk Of The Town
—	The Dreams I Dream	Live At The Talk Of The Town
—	The Day I Met Marie	Live At The Talk Of The Town
—	La La La La La	Live At The Talk Of The Town
—	A Taste Of Honey	Live At The Talk Of The Town
—	Lady Came From Baltimore	Live At The Talk Of The Town
—	When I'm 64	Live At The Talk Of The Town
—	What's More I Don't Need Her	Live At The Talk Of The Town
—	*Medley: The Young Ones*	*Unissued*
—	*Lucky Lips*	*Unissued*
—	*Living Doll*	*Unissued*
—	*In The Country*	*Unissued*
—	Congratulations	Live At The Talk Of The Town
—	Visions	Live At The Talk Of The Town
—	Congratulations – Play Off	Live At The Talk Of The Town

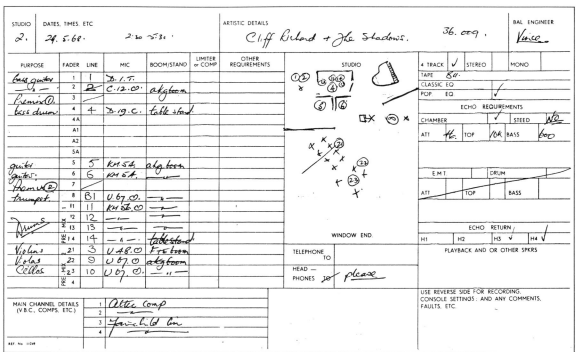

A typical studio layout sheet from Abbey Road.

The Norrie Paramor Orchestra
Vocals: The Breakaways

Producer: Norrie Paramor
Engineer: Peter Vince
Session hours: 10.00 pm–midnight

Two more shows were recorded on 31 May and 1 June with the same titles as recorded here.

Studio session for Columbia
31 May 1968
Abbey Road

—	Don't Forget To Catch Me	Established 1958
—	*What's Behind The Eyes Of Mary*	*Unissued*
—	Ooh La La	Established 1958

Guitars: Hank Marvin
          Bruce Welch
Bass: John Rostill
Drums: Brian Bennett

Producer: Norrie Paramor
Engineer: Peter Vince
Recorded in studio 2
Session hours: 2.30 pm–6.00 pm

Studio session for Columbia
5 June 1968
Abbey Road

04	Somewhere By The Sea	Established 1958

Guitars: Hank Marvin
          Bruce Welch
Bass: John Rostill
Drums: Brian Bennett

Producer: Norrie Paramor
Engineer: Peter Vince / Alan Kane
Recorded in studio 2
Session hours: 2.30 pm–5.30 pm

Studio session for Columbia
10 June 1968
Abbey Road

—	Not The Way It Should Be	Established 1958

Guitars: Hank Marvin
          Bruce Welch
Bass: John Rostill
Drums: Brian Bennett

Producer: Norrie Paramor
Engineer: Peter Vince
Recorded in studio 2
Session hours: 2.30 pm–6.00 pm

Studio session for Columbia
1 July 1968
Abbey Road

—	*The Long Way Home*	*Unissued*
—	What A Silly Thing	Tracks 'n' Grooves
—	Mr Nice	B-side
—	Baby I Could Be So Good At Loving You	Sincerely Cliff

The Mike Leander Orchestra

Producer: Norrie Paramor
Engineer: Peter Vince
Recorded in studio 3
Session hours: 7.00 pm–10.45 pm

Studio session for Columbia
2 July 1968
Chappell Studios

—	As I Walk	Tracks 'n' Grooves
—	In The Past	Sincerely Cliff
—	Marianne	A-side
—	Don't Let Tonight Ever End	Tracks 'n' Grooves
—	What's Behind The Eyes Of Mary	Established 1958

The Mike Leander Orchestra

Producer: Norrie Paramor
Engineer: Peter Vince
Session hours: 7.00 pm–10.00 pm

**Studio session for Columbia
6 July 1968
Abbey Road**

—	Always	Sincerely Cliff
—	Occasional Rain	B-side

The Mike Leander Orchestra

Producer: Norrie Paramor
Engineer: Peter Vince
Recorded in studio 2
Session hours: 7.00 pm–10.00 pm

**Studio session for Columbia
10 October 1968
Abbey Road**

—	Leave My Woman Alone	B-side
—	Will You Love Me Tomorrow	Sincerely Cliff
—	Bang Bang	Tracks 'n' Grooves

The Norrie Paramor Orchestra

Producer: Norrie Paramor
Engineer: Peter Vince
Recorded in studio 2
Session hours: 2.00 pm–5.00 pm

**Studio session for Columbia
24 October 1968
Abbey Road**

—	*If I Do*	*Unissued*
—	*Note In A Bottle*	*Unissued*
—	You Never Can Tell	B-side

The Norrie Paramor Orchestra

Producer: Norrie Paramor
Engineer: Peter Vince
Recorded in studio 1
Session hours: 2.00 pm–4.45 pm

**Studio session for Columbia
31 October 1968
Abbey Road**

—	Wonderful World	German B-side
—	Marianne	German release
—	Geh' Deinen Weg Nicht So Allein (The Dreams I Dream)	German release

The Norrie Paramor Orchestra

Producer: Norrie Paramor
Engineer: Peter Vince
Recorded in studio 2
Session hours: 2.00 pm–5.00 pm

**Studio session for Columbia
20 November 1968
Abbey Road**

—	Twist In Blut (Twist And Shout)	German release
—	Dreizehn Auf Ein Dutzend	German release
—	Die Liebe Ist Immer Nur Heute (I'll Love You Forever Today)	German release

The Norrie Paramor Orchestra

Producer: Norrie Paramor
Engineer: Peter Vince
Recorded in studio 2
Session hours: 2.00 pm–5.00 pm

Studio session for Columbia
27 November 1968
Abbey Road

—	Stell Mich Deinen Eltern Vor (Not The Way That It Should Be)	German release
—	Deine Augen Träumen Mary (What's Behind The Eyes Of Mary)	German release
—	Ooh La La	German release

The Norrie Paramor Orchestra

Producer: Norrie Paramor
Engineer: Peter Vince
Recorded in studio 2
Session hours: 2.00 pm–5.00 pm

Studio session for Columbia
28 November 1968
Abbey Road

—	Zärtliche Sekunden (Don't Forget To Catch Me)	German A-side
—	Shoom Llamma Boom Boom	German release
—	Story Ohne Happy-End (Girl On The Bus)	German release

The Norrie Paramor Orchestra

Producer: Norrie Paramor
Engineer: Peter Vince
Recorded in studio 2
Session hours: 2.00 pm–5.00 pm

Studio sessions for Columbia
2/3 December 1968
Abbey Road

—	*Love Is More Than Words*	*Unissued*
—	*Compassion Road*	*Unissued*
—	*No One Seems To Care*	*Unissued*

—	*Help*	*Unissued*
—	*That's What Love Is*	*Unissued*

Recorded with The Settlers

Producer: Norrie Paramor
Engineer: —
Recorded in studio 3
Session hours: 2.00 pm–5.00 pm

Studio session for Columbia
8/9 January 1969
Abbey Road

—	*Now I've Done It*	*Unissued*
—	*Where Is The Man*	*Unissued*
—	*You Held My Hand*	*Unissued*
—	*Forgive Me*	*Unissued*
—	*Johnny*	*Unissued*
—	*The Fellow Next To Me*	*Unissued*
—	*Don't Blame Me*	*Unissued*
—	*Johnny Wake Up To Reality*	*Unissued*

Recorded with The Settlers

Producer: Norrie Paramor
Engineer: —
Recorded in studio 3
Session hours: 10.00 pm–1.00 am

Studio session for Columbia
11 January 1969
Abbey Road

—	*Turn It Into Cash*	*Unissued*
—	*This Is My Kind Of Love*	*Unissued*
—	*I Will Arise And Go*	*Unissued*
—	*Celebrate*	*Unissued*
—	*Happy World*	*Unissued*
—	*Seeing Is Believing*	*Unissued*
—	*Till Winter Follows Spring*	*Unissued*
—	*Nowhere Man*	*Unissued*

Recorded with The Settlers

Producer: Norrie Paramor
Engineer: —
Recorded in studio 3
Session hours: 2.30 pm–5.30 pm and 7.00 pm–10.00 pm

Studio session for Columbia
31 January 1969
IBC Studios

—	You'll Want Me	Sincerely Cliff
—	I'm Not Getting Married	Sincerely Cliff
—	Good Times	A-side

Mike Vickers Orchestra

Producer: Norrie Paramor
Engineer: Peter Vince
Session hours: 7.00 pm–10.00 pm

Studio session for Columbia
21 February 1969
Abbey Road

—	Relève Mon Defi (Questions)	French release
—	Je Suis Formidable (Two A Penny)	French release

The Norrie Paramor Orchestra

Producer: Norrie Paramor
Engineer: Peter Vince
Recorded in studio 3
Session hours: —

Studio session for Columbia
24 February 1969
Chappell Studios

—	Chi Lo Sa (On The Beach)	Italian B-side
—	Non Dimenticare Chi Ti Ama (Don't Forget To Catch Me)	Italian A-side

The Norrie Paramor Orchestra

Producer: Norrie Paramor
Engineer: Peter Vince
Session hours: 7.00 pm–10.00 pm

Picture bag for single issued in Italy.

Studio session for Columbia
24 March 1969
Abbey Road

—	*Is There An Answer*	*Unissued*
—	*Small World*	*Unissued*
—	*The Carnival's Just For Me*	*Unissued*
—	*Can It Be True*	*Unissued*

Recorded with The Settlers

Producer: Norrie Paramor
Engineer: —
Recorded in studio 3
Session hours: —

Studio session for Columbia
18 April 1969
Abbey Road

—	Sam	Sincerely Cliff
—	So Long	B-side
—	Take Good Care Of Her	Sincerely Cliff

Orchestra: —

Producer: Norrie Paramor
Engineer: Peter Vince
Recorded in studio 2
Session hours: 7.00 pm–10.00 pm

Studio session for Columbia
22 April 1969
Abbey Road

—	My Head Goes Around	Tracks 'n' Grooves
—	Big Ship	A-side
—	When I Find You	Sincerely Cliff

Mike Vickers Orchestra

Producer: Norrie Paramor
Engineer: Peter Vince
Recorded in studio 2
Session hours: 7.00 pm–10.00 pm

Studio session for Columbia
30 April 1969
Abbey Road

—	She's Leaving You	B-side
—	Time Flies	B-side
—	Take Action	Sincerely Cliff

Orchestra: —

Producer: Norrie Paramor
Engineer: Peter Vince / Richard Langham
Recorded in studio 2
Session hours: 7.00 pm–10.00 pm

Studio session for Columbia
2 May 1969
Abbey Road

—	*No Name No Fame*	*Unissued*
—	Throw Down A Line	A-side
—	Early In The Morning	Tracks 'n' Grooves

Mike Vickers Orchestra

Producer: Norrie Paramor
Engineer: Peter Vince
Recorded in studio 2
Session hours: 7.00 pm–10.00 pm

Studio session for Columbia
29 July 1969
Abbey Road

—	Reflections	B-side
—	Love, Truth And Emily Stone	Tracks 'n' Grooves
—	With The Eyes Of A Child	A-side

Mike Vickers Orchestra

Producer: Norrie Paramor
Engineer: Peter Vince
Recorded in studio 2
Session hours: 7.00 pm–10.00 pm

Studio session for Columbia
22 September 1969
Abbey Road

—	Abraham, Martin And John	Tracks 'n' Grooves
—	Your Heart's Not In Your Love	Tracks 'n' Grooves
—	*Love Is Like A Crescendo*	*Unissued*
—	*Postmark Heaven*	*Unissued*
—	Are You Only Fooling Me	Tracks 'n' Grooves
—	*When You Are There*	*Unissued*

Producer: Norrie Paramor
Engineer: Peter Vince
Recorded in studio 2
Session hours: 2.30 pm–5.30 pm and 7.00 pm–10.00 pm

Studio session for Columbia
Dates unknown
Location unknown

—	Ezekiel's Vision	His Land
—	Dry Bones	His Land
—	His Land	His Land
—	Jerusalem, Jerusalem	His Land
—	The New 23rd	His Land
—	His Land	His Land
—	Hava Nagila	His Land

—	Over In Bethlehem	His Land
—	Keep Me Where Love Is	His Land
—	He's Everything To Me	His Land
—	Hallelujah Chorus	His Land

Ralf Carmichael Orchestra
Vocals: Cliff / Cliff Barrows
Chorus: —

Producer: —
Engineer: —
Session hours: —

**Studio session for Columbia
7 January 1970
Advision**

—	The Joy Of Living	A-side

Mike Vickers Orchestra

Producer: Norrie Paramor
Engineer: —
Recorded in studio: —
Session hours: —

**Studio session for Columbia
21 January 1970
Chappell Studios**

—	*Pentecost*	*Unissued*
—	Kein Zug Nach Gretna Green (Gretna Green)	German release
—	Du Du Gefälst Mir So (Green Green)	German release

Producer: Norrie Paramor
Engineer: —
Session hours: 7.00 pm–10.00 pm

**Studio session for Columbia
20 February 1970
Abbey Road**

—	The Birth Of John The Baptist	About That Man
—	Sweet Little Jesus Boy	About That Man
—	The Visit Of The Wise Men	About That Man
—	John The Baptist Points Out Jesus	About That Man
—	Jesus Recruits His Helpers	About That Man
03	Where Is That Man	About That Man
—	Jesus Addresses The Crowd	About That Man
—	Can It Be True	About That Man
—	Jesus Is Betrayed And Arrested	About That Man
—	The Trial Of Jesus	About That Man
—	His Execution And Death	About That Man
—	The First Easter	About That Man
—	Reflections	About That Man

Guitar: —

Producer: Norrie Paramor
Engineer: Richard Langham
Recorded in studio 2
Session hours: 7.00 pm–10.00 pm

**Studio session for Columbia
12 March 1970
Abbey Road**

—	Goodbye Sam, Hello Samantha	A-side
—	I Ain't Got Time Anymore	A-side
—	Monday Comes Too Soon	B-side

Mike Vickers Orchestra

Producer: Norrie Paramor
Engineer: —
Recorded in studio 3
Session hours: 7.30 pm–10.30 pm

Studio session for Columbia
1 June 1970
Abbey Road

—	*The Old Accordion*	*Unissued*
—	*A Sad Song With A Happy Soul*	*Unissued*
—	*I Was Only Fooling Myself*	*Unissued*

Producer: Norrie Paramor
Engineer: —
Recorded in studio 3
Session hours: 7.00 pm–10.00 pm

Studio session for Columbia
29 June 1970
Chappell Studios

| — | Goodbye Sam Das Ist Die Liebe (Goodbye Sam, Hello Samantha) | German A-side |

Producer: Norrie Paramor
Engineer: —
Session hours: 7.00 pm–10.00 pm

Studio session for Columbia
30 June 1970
Abbey Road

| — | *Indifference* | *Unissued* |
| — | *Rain Cloud* | *Unissued* |

Producer: Norrie Paramor
Engineer: —
Recorded in studio 2
Session hours: 7.00 pm–10.00 pm

Studio session for Columbia
16 November 1970
Abbey Road

03	Don't Move Away	B-side
04	I Was Only Fooling Myself	B-side
04	Sunny Honey Girl	A-side

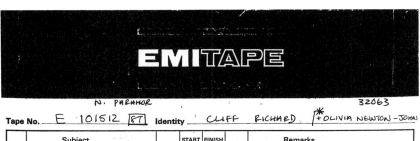

Guitar: —
Bass: —
Drums: —
Piano: —
Organ: —
Acoustic guitar: —
Strings: —
Duet Vocals: Olivia Newton-John on Don't Move Away

Producer: Norrie Paramor
Engineer: Peter Vince / Richard Langham
Recorded in studio 2
Session hours: 7.00 pm–10.00 pm

**Studio session for Columbia
17 November 1970
Abbey Road**

| — | Silvery Rain | A-side |
| — | *Take A Look Around* | *Unissued* |

Producer: Norrie Paramor
Engineers: Peter Vince / Richard Langham
Recorded in studio 3
Session hours: 2.30 pm–5.30 pm

**Studio session for Columbia
24 November 1970
Abbey Road**

—	Umbarella (Annabella Umbrella)	German release
—	Lass Uns Schnell Vergessen (Don't Ask Me To Be Friends)	German release
—	Das Girl Von Nebanan	German release

| — | Du Fragst Mich Immer Wieder | German release |
| — | Wenn Du Lachst, Lacht Das Gluck? (Sally Sunshine) | German release |

Producer: Norrie Paramor
Engineer: —
Recorded in studio 2
Session hours: 2.30 pm–5.30 pm and 7.00 pm–10.00 pm

The backing tracks for the above titles were recorded in Cologne.

**Studio session for Columbia
25 November 1970
Abbey Road**

—	Concerto	German release
—	Neben Dir Wird's Keine Geben (Early In The Morning)	German release
—	Zum Heiraten Bin Ich Kein Typ (I'm Not Getting Married)	German release
—	Der Mann Neben Dir (Baby Don't You Know Anymore)	German release

Producer: Norrie Paramor
Engineer: —
Recorded in studio 2
Session hours: 2.30 pm–5.30 pm and 7.00 pm–10.00 pm

The backing tracks for the above titles were recorded in Germany.

7

Help It Along

1971–1974

───────────────────── **The Records** ─────────────────────

Sunny Honey Girl /		
Don't Move Away	Single	19 / —
Silvery Rain / Annabella Umbrella	Single	27 / —
Flying Machine / Pigeon	Single	37 / —
Sing A Song Of Freedom /		
A Thousand Conversations	Single	13 / —
Jesus / Mr Cloud	Single	35 / —
Living In Harmony /		
Empty Chairs	Single	12 / —
A Brand New Song /		
The Old Accordion	Single	— / —
Power To All Our Friends /		
Come Back Billie Jo	Single	4 / —
Help It Along / Tomorrow Rising	Single	29 / —
Take Me High / Celestial Houses	Single	27 / —
Hangin' On / Love Is Here	Single	13 / —
The Best of Cliff Vol. 2	LP	49
Take Me High	LP	41
Help It Along	LP	
31st Of February Street	LP	

The decline in chart placings continued throughout this period with some singles barely nudging the top twenty and others not even doing that. Of the more successful ones *Sunny Honey Girl* enjoyed moderate sales sending the single to a top twenty position. The next two singles just did not have enough impact to score big on the charts, although the follow-up *Sing A*

Song Of Freedom became the most successful, reaching the number 13 spot and spending more weeks on the chart than any of the previous 1971 singles. 1972 turned out to be another poor year chartwise, with only *Living In Harmony* showing enough promise to chart, as the previous one *Jesus* failed to appeal to a mass audience. A worse fate lay in store for the last single of the year – *Brand New Song* simply went unnoticed and became the first ever Cliff single not to reach the charts, and the first one produced without Norrie Paramor's guidance. However, the following year did show an improvement, with Cliff again representing Britain in the Eurovision Song Contest. *Power To All Our Friends* became his biggest hit since *Congratulations* in 1968, but the two other singles that were released in 1973 were hardly hit records. *Hangin' On*, the only single in 1974, fared slightly better, peaking at number 13.

On the album front matters were not improved. None of the albums reached any higher than the top 40. The soundtrack album from "Take Me High" only did slightly better than THE BEST OF CLIFF VOLUME 2, but considerably worse than previous soundtrack albums, a fate that was to befall the films at the box-office as well.

───────────────────── **The Sessions** ─────────────────────

Studio sessions for EMI: Chappell Studios
Studio sessions for EMI: Abbey Road
Live recordings for EMI: Japan

Take Me High soundtrack sessions: Abbey Road
Studio sessions for EMI: Morgan Studios
Live recordings for EMI: Tokyo, Japan

The February 1971 sessions show a continuation of the line that started in March 1970 with its emphasis on the recording of A and B side material, but surprisingly no album tracks were taped during this time. Besides all the recording activity, 1972 was the year that saw Cliff return to Japan for live work, and from this tour EMI put together an album of live recordings released in the Far East only as LIVE IN JAPAN. As for the musicians backing Cliff, his old pals from the Shadows, Bruce Welch and Hank Marvin appeared with their new partner John Farrar as Marvin, Welch and Farrar. Brian Bennett, another Shadow regular, played drums and was a natural choice as musical director. Alan Hawkshaw was brought in to provide the piano work, and vocal backing came from Olivia Newton-John and Pat Carroll. For the repertoire of the show, a basic set-up was followed with a string of hit material interspersed with some new songs.

Plans were made to follow-up these live recordings with more sessions at Abbey Road. These sessions produced the single *A Brand New Song* and two tracks for the 31ST OF FEBRUARY STREET album. Dave Mackay took over as supervisor of the recording sessions from this point, and given the presence of a different producer the radical change in sound perhaps did not come as a total surprise. More A and B side recordings were taped at the next few sessions, and as had happened before with *Congratulations* Cliff's 1972 Eurovision Song *Power To All Our Friends* had to be recorded in a number of foreign languages for their respective territories.

The last feature film Cliff made was shot in 1973 necessitating soundtrack sessions, although these did not yield any hit songs. It is thought that Cliff put down his vocals at the September recording dates after the rhythm tracks had been completed as far back as May.

For the September 1973 sessions, the Morgan Studios were chosen. The band assembled for the sessions featured a number of musicians that would work for Cliff through to the eighties, people like Terry Britten, Alan Tarney and Trevor Spencer. The sessions lasted over three days and provided all the material for the HELP IT ALONG album, although it is unknown whether some of the tracks were recorded live. Assuming they were, and to provide continuity, it is likely that some of the applause was dubbed in on the studio takes, but we cannot be sure of this as no further information has been logged on the recording sheets.

Cliff returned to Abbey Road to complete tracks for the 31ST OF FEBRUARY STREET album early in 1974. Perhaps as an acknowledgement of the changes that had taken place in the music scene, it was decided to include material of a more contemporary nature, and generally the songs that make up the album are of a high standard, with some being especially impressive in an attempt to produce a concept album.

Following the success of the LIVE IN JAPAN album it seemed the obvious thing to do was to record another live set, aimed again at the Japanese and Far East audiences only. At least two complete shows were recorded by EMI, but of these only items selected for release on the JAPAN TOUR double album were filed with Abbey Road, although these tapes do contain four unissued tracks – *Living In Harmony, Nothing To Remind Me, The Next Time* and *Wind Me Up*. It is unknown why these four were omitted from the album, and one can only assume the reason was likely to have been over-running the duration time of the album.

Studio session for Columbia
12 February 1971
Chappell Studios

Producer: Norrie Paramor
Engineer: —
Session hours: 7.00 pm–10.00 pm

| — | Pigeon | B-side |
| — | Annabella Umbrella | B-side |

Studio session for Columbia
5 March 1971
Chappell Studios

—   *'Cause I Believe In Loving*   *Unissued*
—   *I Who Have Nothing*   *Unissued*

Producer: Norrie Paramor
Engineer: —
Session hours: 7.00 pm–10.00 pm

Studio session for Columbia
20 March 1971
Abbey Road

—   Flying Machine   A-side

Norrie Paramor Orchestra

Producer: Norrie Paramor
Engineer: —
Recorded in studio 3
Session hours: 2.30 pm–5.30 pm

Studio session for Columbia
28 April 1971
Abbey Road

—   Mr Cloud   B-side

Producer: Norrie Paramor
Engineer: —
Recorded in studio: —
Session hours: —

Studio session for Columbia
2 June 1971
Abbey Road

—   La Ballade De Baltimore   French
release
—   L'Amandier Sauvage   French
release

Producer: Norrie Paramor
Engineer: —
Recorded in studio 2
Session hours: 2.30 pm–5.30 pm and
7.00 pm–10.00 pm

Studio session for Columbia
23 August 1971
Abbey Road

—   Kleine Taube   German
(You're My Pigeon)   A-side

Producer: Norrie Paramor
Engineer: —
Recorded in studio 2
Session hours: 2.30 pm–5.30 pm and
7.00 pm–10.00 pm

Studio session for Columbia
24 August 1971
Abbey Road

—   Sing A Song Of Freedom   A-side
—   A Thousand Conversations   B-side

Producer: Norrie Paramor
Engineer: —
Recorded in studio 2
Session hours: 2.30 pm–5.30 pm and
7.00 pm–10.00 pm

Studio session for Columbia
9 September 1971
Abbey Road

—   The Old Accordion   B-side

Producer: Norrie Paramor
Engineer: —
Recorded in studio 1
Session hours: 9.30 pm–10.00 pm

Studio session for Columbia
14 December 1971
Abbey Road

—   Jesus   A-side

Producer: Norrie Paramor
Engineer: —
Recorded in studio 2
Session hours: 7.00 pm–10.00 pm

**Studio session for Columbia
28 April 1972
Abbey Road**

| — | Empty Chairs | B-side |
| — | *Run For Shelter* | *Unissued* |

Guitars: —
—
Bass: —
Drums: —
Piano: —
Vocals: John Farrar / Pat Farrar

Producer: Norrie Paramor
Engineer: —
Recorded in studio 3
Session hours: 2.30 pm–5.30 pm

**Studio session for Columbia
4 July 1972
Abbey Road**

| — | Living In Harmony | A-side |

Guitars: —
—
Bass: —
Drums: —
Keyboards: —
Percussion: —
Vocals: —
Strings: —

Producer: Norrie Paramor
Engineer: —
Recorded in studio 3
Session hours: 2.30 pm–5.30 pm

**Live recordings for EMI
October 1972
Japan**

—	Can't Let You Go	Live In Japan
—	Have A Little Talk With Myself	Live In Japan
—	Sunny Honey Girl	Live In Japan
—	The Minute You're Gone	Live In Japan
—	Flying Machine	Live In Japan
—	The Day I Met Marie	Live In Japan
—	Silvery Rain	Live In Japan
—	My Way	Live In Japan
—	Move It	Live In Japan
—	Living In Harmony	Live In Japan
—	Walk On By / The Look Of Love	Live In Japan
—	Early In The Morning	Live In Japan
—	Goodbye Sam, Hello Samantha	Live In Japan
—	Hit Medley	Live In Japan
—	Congratulations	Live In Japan
—	Rock Medley	Live In Japan
—	Sing A Song Of Freedom	Live In Japan

Hit Medley consists of Living Doll / Bachelor Boy / The Young Ones.

Rock Medley consists of The Girl Can't Help It / Great Balls Of Fire / Lucille / Jailhouse Rock / Good Old Rock 'n' Roll / Do You Wanna Dance.

Guitars: Hank Marvin
          Bruce Welch
Bass: John Farrar
Drums: Brian Bennett
Piano: Alan Hawkshaw
Vocals: Olivia Newton-John / Pat Carroll

Producer: Norrie Paramor
Engineer: —
Session hours: —

Studio session for EMI
11 October 1972
Abbey Road

—	A Brand New Song	A-side
—	The Singer	31st Of February Street
—	Going Away	31st Of February Street

Producer: Dave Mackay
Engineer: Peter Vince
Recorded in studio 3
Session hours: 10.00 pm–1.00 am

Studio session for EMI
27 December 1972
Abbey Road

—	Ashes To Ashes	B-side
—	The Days Of Love	B-side
—	Come Back Billie Jo	B-side

Guitars: —
    —
Bass: —
Drums: —
Keyboards: —
Percussion: —
Vocals: —

Producer: Dave Mackay
Engineer: —
Recorded in studio 2
Session hours: 2.30 pm–5.30 pm and 7.00 pm–10.00 pm

Studio session for EMI
28 December 1972
Abbey Road

—	Help It Along	A-side
—	Power To All Our Friends	A-side
—	Tomorrow Rising	B-side

Guitars: —
    —
Bass: —
Drums: —
Keyboards: —
Percussion: —
Vocals: —

Producer: Dave Mackay
Engineer: —
Recorded in studio: —
Session hours: —

Studio session for EMI
21 March 1973
Abbey Road

—	Gut, Dass Es Freunde Gibt (Power To All Our Friends)	German release

Producer: Dave Mackay
Engineer: —
Recorded in studio: —
Session hours: 7.00 pm–10.00 pm

The original backing track was used for this foreign version.

Studio session for EMI
23 March 1973
Abbey Road

—	Il Faut Chanter La Vie (Power To All Our Friends)	French release
—	Todo El Poder A Los Amigos (Power To All Our Friends)	Spanish release

Producer: Dave Mackay
Engineer: —
Recorded in studio: —
Session hours: 2.30 pm–5.30 pm

The original backing track was used for these foreign versions.

Film soundtrack recordings for Take Me High
26/27 May 1973
Abbey Road

05	Brumburger Duet	Take Me High
03	The Game	Take Me High
01	Anti-Brotherhood of Man	Take Me High
01	Winning	Take Me High
02	It's Only Money	Take Me High
07	Life	Take Me High

Orchestra: —

Producer: Dave Mackay
Engineer: Tony Clark
Recorded in studio 3
Session hours: 10.00 am–1.00 pm and
2.30 pm–5.30 pm

Film soundtrack recordings for Take Me High
28/29 May 1973
Abbey Road

03	Take Me High	Take Me High
05	The Word Is Love	Take Me High
10	Midnight Blue	Take Me High

Orchestra: —

Producer: Dave Mackay
Engineer: Tony Clark
Recorded in studio 3
Session hours: 10.00 am–3.00 pm

The tracks from the above two sessions may be backing tracks only. Vocals were added in September.

Tape operator's detailed recording sheet for TAKE ME HIGH session. Note the comment 'Elstree's tape is in Library', suggesting different film versions to those released on record.

Studio session for EMI
16 August 1973
Abbey Road

| — | *Sweet Loving Ways* | *Unissued* |

Guitars: —
    —
Bass: —
Drums: —
Piano: —

Producer: Dave Mackay
Engineer: —
Recorded in studio 3
Session hours: 10.00 am–1.00 pm

Film soundtrack recordings for
Take Me High
3/4/6 September 1973
Abbey Road

—	Why	Take Me High
—	Brumburger Finale	Take Me High
—	Join The Band	Take Me High

Guitar: —
Steel guitar: —
Bass: —
Drums: —
Saxophone: —
Strings: —

Producer: Dave Mackay
Engineer: Tony Clark
Recorded in studio 3
Session hours: 3: 10.00 am–5.30 pm /
                   7.00 pm–11.00 pm
               4: 10.00 am–2.00 pm /
                   2.30 pm–6.30 pm /
                   7.30 pm–1.30 am

Why recorded with Anthony Andrews.

The incidental music (Hover / Fox Hunt / Ginnette / Parlez Moi D'Amour / Woman Magnificent / Tim Meets Flaxman) was also recorded at this session, probably on 6 September.

Studio sessions for EMI
24/25/26 September 1973
Morgan Studios

—	Mr Businessman	Help It Along
—	*Reflections*	*Unissued*
—	Amazing Grace	Help It Along
—	*Jesus Is My Kind Of People*	*Unissued*
—	Higher Ground	Help It Along
—	Sing A Song Of Freedom	Help It Along
—	Day By Day	Help It Along
—	*I've Got Confidence*	*Unissued*
—	Jesus Loves You	Help It Along
—	Silvery Rain	Help It Along
—	*One Fine Day*	*Unissued*
—	Fire And Rain	Help It Along
—	Yesterday, Today, Forever	Help It Along
—	Jesus	Help It Along
—	*Streets Of London*	*Unissued*
—	Celestial Houses	B-side
—	*Chaser*	*Unissued*

Guitars: Terry Britten
         Kevin Peek
Bass: Alan Tarney
Drums: Trevor Spencer
Keyboards: Cliff Hall
Percussion: Barrie Guard
Orchestra conducted by Barrie Guard

Producer: Dave Mackay
Engineer: —
Session hours: 24: 10.00 am–1.00 pm /
                    2.30 pm–5.30 pm /
                    7.00 pm–10.00 pm
               25: 10.00 am–1.00 pm /
                    2.30 pm–5.30 pm
               26: 10.00 am–1.00 pm /
                    2.30 pm–5.30 pm

Studio session for EMI
28 November 1973
Morgan Studios

—   I'll Love You Forever Today   French release

Producer: Dave Mackay
Engineer: —
Session hours: —

It is unclear whether a new backing track was recorded or if the previous track was used.

Studio session for EMI
11 February 1974
Abbey Road

05	Give Me Back That Old Familiar Feeling	31st Of February Street
02	*You And Me*	*Unissued*
06	Hangin' On	A-side
—	Nothing To Remind Me	31st Of February Street

Guitar: Terry Britten
Acoustic guitar: Kevin Peek
Bass: Alan Tarney
Drums: Trevor Spencer
Keyboards: Cliff Hall
           Dave Macrae
Steel guitar: Gordon Huntley
Percussion: Barrie Guard
           Trevor Spencer
Vocals: Anna Peacock / Jean Hawker / Cliff /
Terry Britten / Alan Tarney / David Mackay
Orchestra conducted by Barrie Guard

Producer: Dave Mackay
Engineer: Tony Clark
Recorded in studio 3
Session hours: 10.30 am–3.00 pm

Studio session for EMI
12 February 1974
Abbey Road

sp	Fireside Song	31st Of February Street
02	*Saturday Night At The Whirl*	*Unissued*
11	Travellin' Light	31st Of February Street
08	You'll Never Know	31st Of February Street
17	Our Love Could Be So Real	31st Of February Street
03	*You*	*Unissued*

Guitar: Terry Britten
Acoustic guitar: Kevin Peek
Bass: Alan Tarney
Drums: Trevor Spencer
Keyboards: Cliff Hall
           Dave Macrae
Steel guitar: Gordon Huntley
Percussion: Barrie Guard
           Trevor Spencer
Saxophone: Bob Bertles
Vocals: Anna Peacock / Jean Hawker / Cliff /
Terry Britten / Alan Tarney / David Mackay
Orchestra conducted by Barrie Guard

Producer: Dave Mackay
Engineer: Tony Clark
Recorded in studio 2
Session hours: 10.30 am–10.30 pm

Studio session for EMI
13 February 1974
Abbey Road

07	The Leaving	31st Of February Street
08	Long Long Time	31st Of February Street

06   Love Is Here   B-side
08   There You Go Again   31st Of
                               February
                               Street

Guitar: Terry Britten
Acoustic guitar: Kevin Peek
Bass: Alan Tarney
Drums: Trevor Spencer
Keyboards: Cliff Hall
          Dave Macrae
Steel guitar: Gordon Huntley
Percussion: Barrie Guard
          Trevor Spencer
Vocals: Anna Peacock / Jean Hawker / Cliff /
Terry Britten / Alan Tarney / David Mackay
Orchestra conducted by Barrie Guard

Producer: Dave Mackay
Engineer: Tony Clark
Recorded in studio 2
Session hours: 10.30 am–10.30 pm

Studio session for EMI
25 February 1974
Abbey Road

—   No Matter What   31st Of
                              February
                              Street

—   31st Of February Street 31st Of
     (Opening)   February
                              Street

—   31st Of February Street 31st Of
     (Closing)   February
                              Street

Guitar: Terry Britten
Acoustic guitar: Kevin Peek
Bass: Alan Tarney
Drums: Trevor Spencer
Keyboards: Cliff Hall
          Dave Macrae
Steel guitar: Gordon Huntley
Percussion: Barrie Guard
          Trevor Spencer

Vocals: Anna Peacock / Jean Hawker / Cliff /
Terry Britten / Alan Tarney / David Mackay
Orchestra conducted by Barrie Guard

Producer: Dave Mackay
Engineer: Tony Clark
Recorded in studio 2
Session hours: 10.30 am–5.30 pm

Studio session for EMI
20 June 1974
Morgan Studios

—   (There's A) Honky Tonk
     Angel   A-side

Guitars: —
         —
Bass: —
Drums: —
Piano: —

Producer: Dave Mackay
Engineer: —
Session hours: 11.00 am–1.00 pm and
2.00 pm–6.00 pm

Studio session for EMI
24 June 1974
Morgan Studios

—   Es Gehören Zwei Zum
     Glücklichsein
     (Hangin' On)   German
                              release

Producer: —
Engineer: —
Session hours: —

Live recordings for EMI
7/8 October 1974
Shinjuku Koseinenkin Tokyo Japan

—   Winning   Japan tour
—   Do You Wanna Dance   Japan tour
—   (You Keep Me) Hangin' On Japan tour
—   Make It Easy On Yourself Japan tour
—   The Sun Ain't Gonna Shine
     Anymore   Japan tour
—   *Living In Harmony*   *Unissued*

—	Get Back	Japan tour
—	Fireside Song	Japan tour
—	Travellin' Light	Japan tour
—	Give Me Back That Old Familiar Feeling	Japan tour
—	Early In The Morning	Japan tour
—	Take Me High	Japan tour
—	Hit Medley	Japan tour
—	Constantly	Japan tour
—	*Nothing To Remind Me*	*Unissued*
—	You've Lost That Lovin' Feelin'	Japan tour
—	Gospel Medley	Japan tour
—	Don't Talk To Him	Japan tour
—	Bachelor Boy	Japan tour
—	Don't Meet The Band	Japan tour
—	Rock Medley	Japan tour
—	Higher Ground	Japan tour
—	Sing A Song Of Freedom	Japan tour
—	Visions	Japan tour
—	Power To All Our Friends	Japan tour
—	*The Next Time*	*Unissued*
—	*Wind Me Up*	*Unissued*

Hit Medley consists of Congratulations / In The Country / Dancing Shoes / The Day I Met Marie / On The Beach / Sing A Song Of Freedom.

Gospel Medley consists of Jesus / Amazing Grace / Jesus Is My Kind Of People.

Rock Medley consists of His Latest Flame / Chantilly Lace / Bonie Moronie / Do You Wanna Dance / Crocodile Rock / Do You Wanna Dance.

Producer: —
Engineer: —
Session hours: —

Publicity shot from the mid 1970s.

8

I'm Nearly Famous

1975–1977

──────────────── **The Records** ────────────────

It's Only Me You've Left Behind/		
You're The One	Single	
Honky Tonk Angel/		
Wouldn't You Know It	Single	
Miss You Nights/Love Is Enough	Single	15/—
Devil Woman/Love On	Single	9/—
I Can't Ask For Anymore		
Than You/Junior Cowboy	Single	17/—
Hey Mr Dream Maker/		
No One Waits	Single	31/—
My Kinda Life/		
Nothing Left For Me To Say	Single	15/—
When Two Worlds Drift Apart/		
That's Why I Love You	Single	46/—
I'm Nearly Famous	LP	5
Every Face Tells A Story	LP	8
40 Golden Greats	LP	1

Both the singles for 1975 *It's Only Me You've Left Behind* and *Honky Tonk Angel* failed to be registered on the chart at all. However, 1976 showed an improved quality of song material that began to be reflected in the chart placings. The most successful of these, *Devil Woman*, reached number 9 and *Miss You Nights* number 15, although matters were not improved by the follow-up singles through to 1977. Only *I Can't Ask For Anymore Than You* culled from the September 1975 sessions and *My Kinda Life* from the EVERY FACE TELLS A STORY album made it into the top twenty.

The picture was definitely better as far as the albums were concerned. Of the three released in this period, all reached the top ten and sales figures showed considerable improvement compared to the immediately preceding years.

Inner cover of 40 GOLDEN GREATS promotional EP.

I'M NEARLY FAMOUS proved to be a total turnaround for Cliff's recording career that through sheer outstanding artistic triumph took an unprecedented upswing. The next album EVERY FACE TELLS A STORY was in fact another strong one, but 40 GOLDEN GREATS was even stronger becoming Cliff's first number 1 album since SUMMER HOLIDAY had hit the top of the album charts in 1963. Although the TV advertised album contained all previously released material, it has proven to be a consistent seller over the years.

Collectors' Notes

Promotional releases provided two items of interest for 1977. The EVERY FACE TELLS A STORY EP (EMI PSR 410) contained selected tracks from the album and was issued to record stores only, as was the 40 GOLDEN GREATS double EP (EMI PSR 414/415) that featured highlights of all 40 tracks.

The Sessions

Studio sessions for EMI: Abbey Road

For the September 1975 sessions at Abbey Road, three songs had been channelled to Cliff through Bruce Welch who as such was producer for *Devil Woman, I Can't Ask For Anymore Than You* and *Miss You Nights.* Collectively these singles showed that Cliff had not only caught up with the contemporary scene, but was breaking new ground as well. Perhaps none of this could have been accomplished without the talented musicians backing Cliff. Men like Terry Britten, Brian Bennett, Graham Todd, Alan Tarney, Clem Cattini and Bob Efford were all experienced pros making them ideal for bringing out Cliff's real strength. Apart from this great line-up of band members and the technical expertise of producer and engineer, there was Tony Rivers who did all the vocal arrangements superbly. But perhaps the most important fact was that Cliff was being offered quality song material again, thanks largely to Bruce Welch.

The decision to follow up these magnificent sessions in December was seen as a desire to make an album in the same vein with the same musicians and technical crew in attendance.

The songs recorded were further explorations of the material taped in September that met with great critical acclaim hailed as "the renaissance of Cliff Richard". Even the more serious music press gave the I'M NEARLY FAMOUS album jubilant reviews. The material offered for recording at the album sessions for EVERY FACE TELLS A STORY was again of a high standard. Of these *Dream Maker, You Got Me Wondering* and *Don't Turn The Light Out* were in a class all of their own. The sessions lasted five days through to September 1976 providing all the tracks needed for the album, and were completed under more or less identical conditions to the I'M NEARLY FAMOUS sessions with the same musicians and technical crew.

A series of sessions in January 1977 was geared towards producing a new inspirational album. The band was virtually the same as the one used during this period with the addition of Bryn Haworth on guitar and Stuart Calver joining Tony Rivers and John Perry on backing vocals. Cliff was credited as producer on all the tracks that made up the SMALL CORNERS album.

Studio session for EMI
27 January 1975
Abbey Road

—	Love Is Enough	B-side
—	It's Only Me You've Left Behind	A-side

Strings: —

Producer: Dave Mackay
Engineer: —
Recorded in studio 3/2
Session hours: 10.00 am–1.00 pm and 7.00 pm–10.00 pm

Studio session for EMI
29 January 1975
Abbey Road

—   You're The One   B-side

Producer: Dave Mackay
Engineer: —
Recorded in studio 2
Session hours: 10.00 am–1.00 pm and
7.00 pm–10.00 pm

Studio session for EMI
29 May 1975
Abbey Road

—   Wouldn't You Know It   B-side

Guitar: Terry Britten
Bass: Alan Tarney
Drums: Brian Bennett
        Clem Cattini
Keyboards: Graham Todd
Saxophone: Steve Gregory
—: Bob Efford
String arrangements by Richard Hewson
Vocals: Tony Rivers / John Perry / A. Harding

Producer: Bruce Welch
Engineer: Tony Clark
Recorded in studio 2
Session hours: 2.30 pm–5.30 pm and
7.00 pm–10.00 pm

Studio session for EMI
8 September 1975
Abbey Road

03   Devil Woman   A-side
05   I Can't Ask For Anymore
        Than You   I'm Nearly
                                     Famous

Guitar: Terry Britten
Bass: Alan Tarney
Drums: Brian Bennett
        Clem Cattini
Keyboards: Graham Todd
Saxophone: Steve Gregory
—: Bob Efford
String arrangements by Richard Hewson
Vocals: Tony Rivers / John Perry / A. Harding

Producer: Bruce Welch
Engineer: Tony Clark
Recorded in studio 2
Session hours: 2.30 pm–6.15 pm and
7.00 pm–10.30 pm

Studio session for EMI
9 September 1975
Abbey Road

11   Miss You Nights   A-side

Guitar: Terry Britten
Bass: Alan Tarney
Drums: Brian Bennett
        Clem Cattini
Keyboards: Graham Todd
Saxophone: Steve Gregory
—: Bob Efford
String arrangements by Richard Hewson
Vocals: Tony Rivers / John Perry / A. Harding

Producer: Bruce Welch
Engineer: Tony Clark
Recorded in studio 2
Session hours: 3.00 pm–5.45 pm and
7.00 pm–10.00 pm

Studio session for EMI
1 December 1975
Abbey Road

04   *I Wish You'd Change Your*
        Mind   *Unissued*
01   You've Got To Give Me All
        Your Lovin'   I'm Nearly
                                     Famous
—   *If You Walked Away*   *Unissued*
03   Alright It's Alright   I'm Nearly
                                     Famous

Guitar: Terry Britten
Bass: Alan Tarney
Drums: Brian Bennett
        Clem Cattini
Keyboards: Graham Todd
Saxophone: Steve Gregory
—: Bob Efford
String arrangements by Richard Hewson
Vocals: Tony Rivers / John Perry / A. Harding

Producer: Bruce Welch
Engineer: Tony Clark
Recorded in studio 3
Session hours: 2.30 pm–5.45 pm and
6.30 pm–7.30 pm

Studio session for EMI
2 December 1975
Abbey Road

05	If You Walked Away	I'm Nearly Famous
03	*Every Face Tells A Story*	*Unissued*
02	I'm Nearly Famous	I'm Nearly Famous
01	*It's No Use Pretending*	*Unissued*

Guitar: Terry Britten
Bass: Alan Tarney
Drums: Brian Bennett
        Clem Cattini
Keyboards: Graham Todd
Saxophone: Steve Gregory
—: Bob Efford
String arrangements by Richard Hewson
Vocals: Tony Rivers / John Perry / A. Harding

Producer: Bruce Welch
Engineer: Tony Clark
Recorded in studio 3
Session hours: 2.30 pm–6.00 pm and
7.00 pm–10.15 pm

Studio session for EMI
3 December 1975
Abbey Road

04	*It's No Use Pretending*	*Unissued*
06	*Lovers*	*Unissued*
—	*Junior Cowboy*	*Unissued*
04	Such Is The Mystery	I'm Nearly Famous

Guitar: Terry Britten
Bass: Alan Tarney
Drums: Brian Bennett
        Clem Cattini
Keyboards: Graham Todd
Saxophone: Steve Gregory
—: Bob Efford

String arrangements by Richard Hewson
Vocals: Tony Rivers / John Perry / A. Harding

Producer: Bruce Welch
Engineer: Tony Clark
Recorded in studio 3
Session hours: 2.30 pm–5.30 pm and
6.30 pm–10.15 pm

Studio session for EMI
4 December 1975
Abbey Road

11	Junior Cowboy	B-side
06	I Wish You'd Change Your Mind	I'm Nearly Famous
08	Lovers	I'm Nearly Famous

Guitar: Terry Britten
Bass: Alan Tarney
Drums: Brian Bennett
        Clem Cattini
Keyboards: Graham Todd
Saxophone: Steve Gregory
—: Bob Efford
String arrangements by Richard Hewson
Vocals: Tony Rivers / John Perry / A. Harding

Producer: Bruce Welch
Engineer: Tony Clark
Recorded in studio 3
Session hours: 2.30 pm–6.00 pm and
6.45 pm–9.00 pm

Studio session for EMI
10 December 1975
Abbey Road

06	It's No Use Pretending	I'm Nearly Famous

Guitar: Terry Britten
Bass: Alan Tarney
Drums: Brian Bennett
        Clem Cattini
Keyboards: Graham Todd
Saxophone: Steve Gregory
—: Bob Efford

String arrangements by Richard Hewson
Vocals: Tony Rivers / John Perry / A. Harding

Producer: Bruce Welch
Engineer: Tony Clark
Recorded in studio 3
Session hours: 2.15 pm–5.45 pm and
6.30 pm–midnight

Studio session for EMI
11 December 1975
Abbey Road

06   *Miss You Nights*   *Unissued*

Producer: Bruce Welch
Engineer: Tony Clark
Recorded in studio 3
Session hours: 10.00 pm–12.00 pm

This was a remake for ITV.

Studio session for EMI
25 March 1976
Abbey Road

03   Love On   B-side

Guitar: Terry Britten
Bass: Alan Tarney
Drums: Brian Bennett
        Clem Cattini
Keyboards: Graham Todd
Saxophone: Steve Gregory
—: Bob Efford
String arrangements by Richard Hewson
Vocals: Tony Rivers / John Perry / A. Harding

Producer: Bruce Welch
Engineer: Tony Clark
Recorded in studio 3
Session hours: 10.00 pm–1.45 am

Studio session for EMI
6 September 1976
Abbey Road

03   Try A Smile   Every Face
                                     Tells A
                                     Story

—   *Give Me Love Your Way*   *Unissued*
04   *Too Late To Say Goodbye*   *Unissued*
01   *Part Of Me*   *Unissued*
03   *Don't Turn The Light Out*   *Unissued*

Guitar: Terry Britten
Bass: Alan Tarney
Drums: Brian Bennett
Keyboards: Graham Todd
Percussion: Brian Bennett
            Frank Ricotti
Vocals: Cliff / Tony Rivers / John Perry
Strings arranged by Richard Hewson

Producer: Bruce Welch
Engineer: Tony Clark
Recorded in studio 2
Session hours: 10.00 am–2.00 pm /
3.00 pm–7.00 pm and 8.00 pm–10.00 pm

Main entrance to Abbey Road Studios in North London.
(Photo taken in 1990).

Studio session for EMI
7 September 1976
Abbey Road

03	Don't Turn The Light Out	Every Face Tells A Story
14	Give Me Love Your Way	Every Face Tells A Story
08	Spider Man	Every Face Tells A Story
05	When Two Worlds Drift Apart	Every Face Tells A Story

Guitar: Terry Britten
Bass: Alan Tarney
Drums: Brian Bennett
Keyboards: Graham Todd
Percussion: Brian Bennett
            Frank Ricotti
Vocals: Cliff / Tony Rivers / John Perry
Strings arranged by Richard Hewson

Producer: Bruce Welch
Engineer: Tony Clark
Recorded in studio 2
Session hours: 11.00 am–midnight

Studio session for EMI
8 September 1976
Abbey Road

07	Joseph	Small Corners
03	It'll Be Me Babe	Every Face Tells A Story
—	*Dream Maker*	*Unissued*

Guitar: Terry Britten
Bass: Alan Tarney
Drums: Brian Bennett
Keyboards: Graham Todd
Percussion: Brian Bennett
            Frank Ricotti
Vocals: Cliff / Tony Rivers / John Perry
Strings arranged by Richard Hewson

Producer: Bruce Welch
Engineers: Peter Vince / Tony Clark
Recorded in studio 2
Session hours: 11.00 am–10.00 pm

Studio session for EMI
9 September 1976
Abbey Road

05	*Dream Maker*	*Unissued*
13	Must Be Love	Every Face Tells A Story

Guitar: Terry Britten
Bass: Alan Tarney
Drums: Brian Bennett
Keyboards: Graham Todd
Percussion: Brian Bennett
            Frank Ricotti
Vocals: Cliff / Tony Rivers / John Perry
Strings arranged by Richard Hewson

Producer: Bruce Welch
Engineer: Tony Clark
Recorded in studio 2
Session hours: 10.30 am–10.30 pm

Studio session for EMI
10 September 1976
Abbey Road

03	You Got Me Wondering	Every Face Tells A Story
09	*Every Face Tells A Story*	*Unissued*
—	*Part Of Me*	*Unissued*

Guitar: Terry Britten
Bass: Alan Tarney
Drums: Brian Bennett
Keyboards: Graham Todd
Percussion: Brian Bennett
            Frank Ricotti
Vocals: Cliff / Tony Rivers / John Perry
Strings arranged by Richard Hewson

Producer: Bruce Welch
Engineer: Tony Clark
Recorded in studio 2
Session hours: 10.30 am–10.30 pm

Studio session for EMI
17 September 1976
Abbey Road

04   No One Waits   B-side

Guitar: Terry Britten
Bass: Alan Tarney
Drums: Brian Bennett
Keyboards: Graham Todd
Percussion: Brian Bennett
                Frank Ricotti
Vocals: Cliff / Tony Rivers / John Perry
Strings arranged by Richard Hewson

Producer: Bruce Welch
Engineer: Tony Clark
Recorded in studio 2
Session hours: 10.00 am–11.00 pm

Studio session for EMI
18 September 1976
Abbey Road

02   Mr Dream Maker   Every Face
                                                Tells A
                                                Story

07   Every Face Tells A Story   Every Face
                                                Tells A
                                                Story

Guitar: Terry Britten
Bass: Alan Tarney
Drums: Brian Bennett
Keyboards: Graham Todd
Percussion: Brian Bennett
                Frank Ricotti
Vocals: Cliff / Tony Rivers / John Perry
Strings arranged by Richard Hewson

Producer: Bruce Welch
Engineer: Tony Clark
Recorded in studio 2
Session hours: 10.00 am–10.00 pm

Studio session for EMI
22 September 1976
Abbey Road

05   That's Why I Love You   B-side
03   Nothing Left To Say   B-side

Guitar: Terry Britten
Bass: Alan Tarney
Drums: Brian Bennett
Keyboards: Graham Todd
Percussion: Brian Bennett
                Frank Ricotti
Vocals: Cliff / Tony Rivers / John Perry
Strings arranged by Richard Hewson

Producer: Bruce Welch
Engineer: Peter Vince
Recorded in studio 2
Session hours: 10.00 am–10.30 pm

Studio session for EMI
24 September 1976
Abbey Road

07   Up In The World   Every Face
                                                Tells A
                                                Story

Guitar: Terry Britten
Bass: Alan Tarney
Drums: Brian Bennett
Keyboards: Graham Todd
Percussion: Brian Bennett
                Frank Ricotti
Vocals: Cliff / Tony Rivers / John Perry
Strings arranged by Richard Hewson

Producer: Bruce Welch
Engineer: Tony Clark
Recorded in studio 2
Session hours: 10.00 am–11.30 pm

Studio session for EMI
10 January 1977
Abbey Road

—   My Kinda Life   A-side

Guitar: Mo Witham
Bass: Alan Jones
Drums: Roger Pope
Keyboards: Alan Hawkshaw
Vocals: Cliff / Tony Rivers / John Perry

Producer: Bruce Welch
Engineer: Tony Clark
Recorded in studio 2
Session hours: —

Studio session for EMI
17 January 1977
Abbey Road

03	Going Home	Small Corners
02	Up In Canada	Small Corners
01	News For You	Small Corners
03	Why Should The Devil Have All The Good Music	Small Corners

Guitars: Terry Britten
          Bryn Haworth
Bass: Alan Tarney
Drums: Brian Bennett
Percussion: Brian Bennett
Keyboards: Graham Todd
Vocals: Tony Rivers / John Perry / Stuart Calver

Producer: Cliff Richard
Engineer: Tony Clark
Recorded in studio 3
Session hours: 10.00 am–10.00 pm

Studio session for EMI
18 / 19 January 1977
Abbey Road

03	Why Me Lord	Small Corners
01	Yes He Lives	A-side
06	*You Can't Get To Heaven…*	*Unissued*
—	When I Survey The Wondrous Cross	Small Corners

RECORDING SHEET   Job No. 95727 D

BREAKS 13:30-14.00 + 18.00 - 19.00.

ARTISTIC INFORMATION			COSTING INFORMATION		
Dolby ✓	Artist	Date 18th January 1972	Session Booked Time 10.00 - 22.00		Materials Used
24T ✓ / 16T	CLIFF RICHARD	Location Studio Three	Recording/SI 10.00 - 13.00		1 × 8752ᵃ
8T / 4T		Engineers A.C. H.BAK	Remixing		
2T / Mono		Producer Cliff Richard	Copying		
Quad.			Playback	Editing	

REEL NOS.	TITLES	False Starts	Take Nos.	TAKE DETAILS From	To	DUR.	REMARKS
16 962 D6	WHY ME LORD!		1-3				TAKE 3 BEST
	YES HE LIVES		1	COMPLETE			BEST
	YOU CAN'T GET TO HEAVEN BY LIVING LIKE HELL-5		6	COMPLETE.			BEST
	WHEN I SURVEY!			COMPLETE			BEST 1 GTR / CLAVINET
	WHY SHOULD THE DEVIL						1ST GTR / CLAVINET.
	UP IN CANADA.						

Ref. No 9864A | Abbey Road

Recording sheet from 18 January session. Note error on date.

Guitars: Terry Britten
　　　　　Bryn Haworth
Bass: Alan Tarney
Drums: Brian Bennett
Percussion: Brian Bennett
Keyboards: Graham Todd
Vocals: Tony Rivers / John Perry / Stuart Calver

Producer: Cliff Richard
Engineer: Tony Clark
Recorded in studio 3
Session hours: 10.00 am–1.00 am

Studio session for EMI
19 January 1977
Abbey Road

04	I Wish We'd All Been Ready	Small Corners
03	Hey Watcha Say	Small Corners
02	Good On The Sally Army	Small Corners
03	I Love	Small Corners

Guitars: Terry Britten
　　　　　Bryn Haworth
Bass: Alan Tarney
Drums: Brian Bennett
Percussion: Brian Bennett
Vocals: Tony Rivers / John Perry / Stuart Calver

Producer: Cliff Richard
Engineer: Tony Clark
Recorded in studio 3
Session hours: 11.00 am–10.00 pm

Studio session for EMI
30 March 1977
Abbey Road

| — | Imagine Love | B-side |

Producer: Bruce Welch
Engineer: Tony Clark
Recorded in studio 2
Session hours: —

Studio session for EMI
11 July 1977
Abbey Road

—	I Can't Take The Hurt Anymore	A-side
—	Needing A Friend	B-side
—	*Mobile Alabama School Leaving Hullaballoo*	*Unissued*

Guitars: Terry Britten
　　　　　Tim Renwick
　　　　　Alan Parker
　　　　　Alan Tarney
Bass: Alan Tarney
　　　　Alan Jones
Drums: Brian Bennett
　　　　　Trevor Spencer
Percussion: Brian Bennett
　　　　　　　Trevor Spencer
Keyboards: Graham Todd
　　　　　　Alan Tarney
　　　　　　Duncan Mackay
Vocals: Tony Rivers / John Perry / Stuart Calver / Alan Tarney / Cliff
String arrangements by Richard Hewson

Producer: Bruce Welch
Engineer: Tony Clark
Recorded in studio 3
Session hours: —

9

Rock 'n' Roll Juvenile

1978–1980

─────────────────── **The Records** ───────────────────

Yes He Lives /		
Good On The Sally Army	Single	
Please Remember Me /		
Please Don't Tease	Single	
Can't Take The Hurt Anymore /		
Needing A Friend	Single	
Green Light / Imagine Love	Single	57 / —
We Don't Talk Anymore /		
Count Me Out	Single	1 / —
Hot Shot / Walking In The Light	Single	46 / —
Carrie / Moving In	Single	4 / —
Dreamin' / Dynamite	Single	8 / —
Suddenly /		
You Made Me Love You	Single	15 / —
Small Corners	LP	33
Green Light	LP	25
Thank You Very Much	LP	5
Rock 'n' Roll Juvenile	LP	3
I'm No Hero	LP	4

and *Suddenly*, a duet with Olivia Newton-John from the film soundtrack of "Xanadu", peaked at number 15.

Sales of the 1979 live album were considerably better than the two released in 1978. THANK YOU VERY MUCH contained the recordings made of the 20th Anniversary reunion concerts at the London Palladium with the Shadows. For the repertoire of the shows, the basic set-up as used before was followed – namely a string of hits interspersed with some new songs. The old hits were mainly drawn from sixties repertoire, while for new material, naturally the recent hit *Devil Woman* was chosen as well as *Miss You Nights*, 'The song I haven't left out of any of my concerts since the first time I recorded it in 1975'. The follow-up album, ROCK 'N' ROLL JUVENILE, outdid all

In 1978 both singles and album chart placings seemed all too grim, as illustrated by the fact that not one single reached the top 40. Even if *Green Light* and *Hot Shot*, released the following year, sold slightly better, their peaking at number 57 and 46 respectively hardly made them hit records. However, the one that did make it to the top of the charts became Cliff's first number 1 since 1968 and his biggest selling single with sales just under 3 million worldwide. *We Don't Talk Anymore* stayed on the charts for 14 weeks. All the singles that were released in 1980 reached the top twenty, with *Carrie* achieving the most impressive chart placing at number 4, followed by *Dreamin'* at number 8,

Hank, Cliff and Bruce during rehearsals for the THANK YOU VERY MUCH reunion concert 1978.

the other albums of this period by reaching the number 3 spot and staying on the chart for 22 weeks. It had two top-four singles to spur interest – *Carrie* and *We Don't Talk Anymore*. The successor, I'M NO HERO, released in 1980, turned out to be another big seller and although this time there were no hit singles to boost sales, the album did very well by reaching number 4 and staying on the charts for 11 weeks.

The Sessions

Studio sessions for EMI: Abbey Road
Studio sessions for EMI: Pathé Marconi Studios, Paris
Studio sessions for EMI: RG Jones
Studio sessions for EMI: Los Angeles
Studio sessions for EMI: Riverside Studios

For the January 1978 sessions that ran through to April, Bruce Welch again landed himself the job of producer, providing material for the GREEN LIGHT album. The band was virtually identical to the one used on SMALL CORNERS and EVERY FACE TELLS A STORY, and again featured Shadows drummer Brian Bennett. An intriguing item from these sessions was the new version of Cliff's 1960 hit *Please Don't Tease* that turned up on the B-side of *Please Remember Me*, but somehow never quite matched the greatness of the original recording.

To collect sufficient material for an album, EMI recorded the afternoon and evening shows

Cliff and Olivia during the filming of the *Suddenly* promo.

on 4 March at the London Palladium, when Cliff and the Shadows were reunited on stage for the first time in ten years, recreating the special magic of their twenty-year musical history. Bruce Welch supervised all aspects of the recording and technical work as producer, and although it is not clear how directly Cliff was involved with repair work on these recordings, it is certain that Bruce conducted a string of overdubbing and mixing sessions at Abbey Road, doing a lot of work on the tapes through to December to make the resulting THANK YOU VERY MUCH album a very impressive item.

The April 1978 sessions produced two additional tracks for the GREEN LIGHT album with the same crew and band in attendance as for January.

For the sessions that produced the ROCK 'N' ROLL JUVENILE material, the Pathé Marconi Studio was chosen. Two different recording occasions in July 1978 and again in January 1979 were needed to complete the tracks. The band featured the usual regulars, while new musicians included Herbie Flowers and Tristan Fry from "Sky", and Peter Skellern, a singer–songwriter who had a top ten hit with *You're A Lady*, were brought in to help out. Producer credits were shared between Cliff and Terry Britten. This was the songwriter–musician who had worked on a number of Cliff's recording sessions, and of course had penned *Miss You Nights* and *Devil Woman*.

Plans were made to follow up these overall successful sessions with another at RG Jones Recording Studios in Wimbledon. This took place in May. Bruce Welch had already selected the song, and of course produced the Alan Tarney composition *We Don't Talk Anymore* as Cliff's best selling single of his career. For whatever reason, the session that produced the *Suddenly* track, duetted with Olivia Newton-John, appears to have been recorded in a garage located in Los Angeles. Obviously the acoustics in this improvised studio presented serious problems with traffic noise levels outside. Compounding the technical problems was the recording method used of Cliff and Olivia taping their vocals simultaneously onto a pre-recorded backing track. It is thought Olivia returned at a later date to re-record her vocal due to her track containing the noise levels mentioned above. We cannot trace the origin of the backing track or the musicians featured.

The songs Cliff was to record at the Riverside Studios at his final session of 1980 provided the material for the I'M NO HERO album. Unfortunately we have not been able to track down the names of the musicians on these sessions, but it seems likely they were the same as Cliff had been using over this period.

Studio session for EMI
9 January 1978
Abbey Road

| 02 | Under Lock And Key | Green Light |
| 03 | Ease Along | Green Light |

Guitars: Terry Britten
       Tim Renwick
       Alan Parker
       Alan Tarney
Bass: Alan Tarney
       Alan Jones
Drums: Brian Bennett
       Trevor Spencer
Percussion: Brian Bennett
       Trevor Spencer
Keyboards: Graham Todd
       Alan Tarney
       Duncan Mackay
Vocals: Tony Rivers / John Perry / Stuart Calver / Alan Tarney / Cliff
String arrangements by Richard Hewson

Producer: Bruce Welch
Engineer: Tony Clark
Recorded in studio 3
Session hours: 10.00 am–6.45 pm

Studio session for EMI
10 January 1978
Abbey Road

| 02 | Please Remember Me | A-side |
| *01* | *Ships That Pass In The Night* | *Unissued* |

Guitars: Terry Britten
       Tim Renwick
       Alan Parker
       Alan Tarney

Bass: Alan Tarney
       Alan Jones
Drums: Brian Bennett
       Trevor Spencer
Percussion: Brian Bennett
       Trevor Spencer
Keyboards: Graham Todd
       Alan Tarney
       Duncan Mackay
Vocals: Tony Rivers / John Perry / Stuart Calver / Alan Tarney / Cliff
String arrangements by Richard Hewson

Producer: Bruce Welch
Engineer: Tony Clark
Recorded in studio 3
Session hours: 10.30 am–6.30 pm

Studio session for EMI
11 January 1978
Abbey Road

| 04 | Free My Soul | Green Light |
| *02* | *Muddy Water* | *Unissued* |

Guitars: Terry Britten
       Tim Renwick
       Alan Parker
       Alan Tarney
Bass: Alan Tarney
       Alan Jones
Drums: Brian Bennett
       Trevor Spencer
Percussion: Brian Bennett
       Trevor Spencer
Keyboards: Graham Todd
       Alan Tarney
       Duncan Mackay

Vocals: Tony Rivers / John Perry / Stuart Calver /
Alan Tarney / Cliff
String arrangements by Richard Hewson

Producer: Bruce Welch
Engineer: Tony Clark
Recorded in studio 3
Session hours: 10.30 am–7.00 pm

Studio session for EMI
12 January 1978
Abbey Road

| 01 | Never Even Thought | Green Light |
| 01 | *Do What You Gotta Do* | *Unissued* |

Guitars: Terry Britten
       Tim Renwick
       Alan Parker
       Alan Tarney
Bass: Alan Tarney
      Alan Jones

Drums: Brian Bennett
       Trevor Spencer
Percussion: Brian Bennett
       Trevor Spencer
Keyboards: Graham Todd
       Alan Tarney
       Duncan Mackay
Vocals: Tony Rivers / John Perry / Stuart Calver /
Alan Tarney / Cliff
String arrangements by Richard Hewson

Producer: Bruce Welch
Engineer: Tony Clark
Recorded in studio 3
Session hours: 10.30 am–6.30 pm

Studio session for EMI
13 January 1978
Abbey Road

| 03 | While She's Young | Green Light |

RECORDING SHEET

Job No. *95948P*

BREAK 13:30 – 14:00

ARTISTIC INFORMATION			COSTING INFORMATION		
Dolby ✓	Artist	Date *11–1–78*	Session Booked Time *10:00 – 17:30*	Materials Used
24T ✓ 16T		Location *Studio 3*	Recording/SI *10:30 – 19:00*	*2x Amper*
8T 4T	*CLIFF RICHARD*	Engineers *A.C. H.B.*	Remixing	*G.M. 2"*
2T Mono		Producer *Bruce Welch*	Copying	
Quad.			Playback Editing	

REEL NOS.	TITLES	False Starts	Take Nos.	TAKE DETAILS From	To	DUR.	REMARKS
21263 24T	*PREVIOUS MATERIAL ON THIS TAPE ERASED*						
	FREE MY SOUL		1–4				*4 BEST*
							Pno/Dx
21265 24T	*MUDDY WATER*		1–2				*T2 BEST*
21266 24T			3				

Ref. No 9864A   Abbey Road

Recording sheet from 11 January session. Note comments on previous material erased. Unknown whether Cliff or other
artist(s).

Guitars: Terry Britten
       Tim Renwick
       Alan Parker
       Alan Tarney
Bass: Alan Tarney
       Alan Jones
Drums: Brian Bennett
       Trevor Spencer
Percussion: Brian Bennett
       Trevor Spencer
Keyboards: Graham Todd
       Alan Tarney
       Duncan Mackay
Vocals: Tony Rivers / John Perry / Stuart Calver /
Alan Tarney / Cliff
String arrangements by Richard Hewson

Producer: Bruce Welch
Engineer: Tony Clark
Recorded in studio 3
Session hours: 10.30 am–4.40 pm

Studio session for EMI
14 January 1978
Abbey Road

01	*Gettin' The Feelin'*	*Unissued*
05	Please Don't Tease	B-side
—	Start All Over Again	Green Light

Guitars: Terry Britten
       Tim Renwick
       Alan Parker
       Alan Tarney
Bass: Alan Tarney
       Alan Jones
Drums: Brian Bennett
       Trevor Spencer
Percussion: Brian Bennett
       Trevor Spencer
Keyboards: Graham Todd
       Alan Tarney
       Duncan Mackay
Vocals: Tony Rivers / John Perry / Stuart Calver /
Alan Tarney / Cliff
String arrangements by Richard Hewson

Producer: Bruce Welch
Engineer: Tony Clark
Recorded in studio 3
Session hours: 2.00 pm–7.00 pm

Studio session for EMI
15 January 1978
Abbey Road

02	Count Me Out	Green Light

Guitars: Terry Britten
       Tim Renwick
       Alan Parker
       Alan Tarney
Bass: Alan Tarney
       Alan Jones
Drums: Brian Bennett
       Trevor Spencer
Percussion: Brian Bennett
       Trevor Spencer
Keyboards: Graham Todd
       Alan Tarney
       Duncan Mackay
Vocals: Tony Rivers / John Perry / Stuart Calver /
Alan Tarney / Cliff
String arrangements by Richard Hewson

Producer: Bruce Welch
Engineer: Tony Clark
Recorded in studio 3
Session hours: 3.00 pm–9.00 pm

Studio session for EMI
27 January 1978
Abbey Road

—	*Under Lock And Key*	*Unissued*

Guitars: Terry Britten
       Tim Renwick
       Alan Parker
       Alan Tarney
Bass: Alan Tarney
       Alan Jones
Drums: Brian Bennett
       Trevor Spencer
Percussion: Brian Bennett
       Trevor Spencer
Keyboards: Graham Todd
       Alan Tarney
       Duncan Mackay
Vocals: Tony Rivers / John Perry / Stuart Calver /
Alan Tarney / Cliff
String arrangements by Richard Hewson

Producer: Bruce Welch
Engineer: Tony Clark
Recorded in studio 3
Session hours: 10.00 am–5.30 pm

Live recordings for EMI
4 March 1978
London Palladium

—	The Young Ones	Thank You Very Much
—	Do You Wanna Dance	Thank You Very Much
—	The Day I Met Marie	Thank You Very Much
—	Please Don't Tease	Thank You Very Much
—	Miss You Nights	Thank You Very Much
—	Move It	Thank You Very Much
—	Willie And The Hand Jive	Thank You Very Much
—	All Shook Up	Thank You Very Much
—	*Up In Canada*	*Unissued*
—	*Yes He Lives*	*Unissued*
—	Devil Woman	Thank You Very Much
—	Why Should The Devil Have All The Good Music	Thank You Very Much
—	End Of The Show	Thank You Very Much

Guitars: Hank Marvin
          Bruce Welch
Bass: Alan Jones
Drums: Brian Bennett
Keyboards: Cliff Hall
Guitars: Terry Britten
          Dave Christopher
          Graham Murray
Bass: Mo Foster

RECORDING SHEET

Job No. 96068

BREAKS 1330–1430

ARTISTIC INFORMATION			COSTING INFORMATION		

Dolby: 2 4T, 8T, 2T ✓ Mono ✓, Quad.

Artist: CLIFF + THE SHAD'S. (LONDON PALLADIUM)

Date: 4.12.78
Location: NO 2.
Engineers: PV. AR.
Producer: B. WELCH -

Session Booked Time: 10.00 – 22.00
Recording/SI:
Remixing: 10.00 – 22.00
Copying:
Playback 22.00 – 22.30   Editing:

Materials Used: 2 x 816¼

REEL NOS.	TITLES	False Starts	Take Nos.	TAKE DETAILS From	TAKE DETAILS To	DUR.	REMARKS
	THE YOUNG ONES		CS1	COMPLETE		BEST	
	DO YOU WANNA DANCE		RS1	— " —			
			RS2	— " —			
			RS3	— " —		BEST	
			RS4	GTR SOLOS ONLY			
			RS5	— " —		BEST	
	THE DAY I MET MARIE		RS1	COMPLETE			
			RS2	— " —		BEST	

Ref. No 9864A   Abbey Road

Recording sheet showing work carried out on London Palladium tapes.

Keyboards: Graham Todd
Drums: Graham Jarvis
      Clem Cattini
Vocals: Tony Rivers / Stuart Calver / John Perry

Producer: Bruce Welch
Engineer: Tony Clark
Session hours: —

The afternoon and evening shows were recorded and the above tracks probably came from both shows.

Studio session for EMI
17 April 1978
Abbey Road

01   (Searching For A) Green
      Light   Green Light

Guitars: Terry Britten
       Tim Renwick
       Alan Parker
       Alan Tarney

Bass: Alan Tarney
     Alan Jones
Drums: Brian Bennett
      Trevor Spencer
Percussion: Brian Bennett
           Trevor Spencer
Keyboards: Graham Todd
          Alan Tarney
          Duncan Mackay
Vocals: Tony Rivers / John Perry / Stuart Calver / Alan Tarney / Cliff
String arrangements by Richard Hewson

Producer: Bruce Welch
Engineer: Tony Clark
Recorded in studio 3
Session hours: 2.30 pm – 11.00 pm

RECORDING SHEET

Job No. 95948P

	ARTISTIC INFORMATION				COSTING INFORMATION			
Dolby ✓	Artist			Date 17th May 1978	Session Booked Time 10:00–22:00		Materials Used	
24T ✓ 16T				Location Studio Three	Recording/SI 11:00–22:00			
8T 4T	CLIFF RICHARD			Engineers P.V H.B.	Remixing 10:00–11:00		1 x 8 6¼	
2T ✓ Mono				Producer Bruce Welch	Copying			
Quad.					Playback	Editing		

REEL NOS.	TITLES	False Starts	Take Nos.	TAKE DETAILS From	To	DUR.	REMARKS
22535D2	PLEASE DONT TEASE						Backing TK mixed
21263D24T	FREE MY SOUL						to O/DS
21268D24T	WHILE SHE'S YOUNG						"
21266D24T	NEVER EVEN THOUGHT						"
22971D24T	SEARCHING FOR A GREEN LIGHT						"
21268D24T	START ALL OVER AGAIN						Yamaha Syn # C/DS
21263D24T	FREE MY SOUL						Piano O/DS

Ref. No 9864A   Abbey Road

Recording sheet detailing overdub session for GREEN LIGHT album material.

Studio session for EMI
18 April 1978
Abbey Road

01   She's A Gypsy   Green Light

Guitars: Terry Britten
        Tim Renwick
        Alan Parker
        Alan Tarney
Bass: Alan Tarney
     Alan Jones
Drums: Brian Bennett
       Trevor Spencer
Percussion: Brian Bennett
           Trevor Spencer
Keyboards: Graham Todd
          Alan Tarney
          Duncan Mackay
Vocals: Tony Rivers / John Perry / Stuart Calver /
Alan Tarney / Cliff
String arrangements by Richard Hewson

Producer: Bruce Welch
Engineer: Tony Clark
Recorded in studio 3
Session hours: 11.30 am–midnight

Studio sessions for EMI
18–20 July 1978
Pathé Marconi, Paris

—	Walking In The Light	B-side
—	Monday Thru Friday	Rock 'n' Roll Juvenile
—	Doing Fine	Rock 'n' Roll Juvenile
—	Sci-Fi	Rock 'n' Roll Juvenile
—	You Know That I Love You	Rock 'n' Roll Juvenile
—	Falling In Love	Rock 'n' Roll Juvenile

Guitar: Terry Britten
Bass: Herbie Flowers
Drums: Graham Jarvis
Keyboards: Billy Livesy
Percussion: Tristan Fry
Mellotron: Peter Skellern
Slide guitar: Bryn Haworth
Saxophone: Martin Dobson
Brass: Mel Collins / Martin Drover / Chris Mercer
Vocals: Cliff / Terry Britten / Madelaine Bell

Producers: Cliff Richard / Terry Britten
Engineers: Tony Clark / Haydn Bendall
Session hours: —

Studio sessions for EMI
7–21 January 1979
Pathé Marconi, Paris

—	Hot Shot	Rock 'n' Roll Juvenile
—	Carrie	Rock 'n' Roll Juvenile
—	Language of Love	Rock 'n' Roll Juvenile
—	Cities May Fall	Rock 'n' Roll Juvenile
—	My Luck Won't Change	Rock 'n' Roll Juvenile
—	*Rock 'n' Roll Juvenile*	*Unissued*

Guitar: Terry Britten
Bass: Herbie Flowers
Drums: Graham Jarvis
Keyboards: Billy Livesy
Percussion: Tristan Fry
Mellotron: Peter Skellern
Slide guitar: Bryn Haworth
Saxophone: Martin Dobson
Brass: Mel Collins / Martin Drover / Chris Mercer
Vocals: Cliff / Terry Britten / Madelaine Bell

Producers: Cliff Richard / Terry Britten
Engineers: Tony Clark / Haydn Bendall
Session hours: —

Studio session for EMI
24 January 1979
Abbey Road

04	Rock 'n' Roll Juvenile	Rock 'n' Roll Juvenile

Guitar: Terry Britten
Bass: Herbie Flowers
Drums: Graham Jarvis
Keyboards: Billy Livesy
Percussion: Tristan Fry
Mellotron: Peter Skellern
Slide guitar: Bryn Haworth
Saxophone: Martin Dobson
Brass: Mel Collins / Martin Drover / Chris Mercer
Vocals: Cliff / Terry Britten / Madelaine Bell

Producers: Cliff Richard / Terry Britten
Engineers: Tony Clark / Haydn Bendall
Recorded in studio 3
Session hours: midday–10.00 pm

Studio session for EMI
29 May 1979
RG Jones

03	We Don't Talk Any More	A-side

Guitars: Alan Tarney
        Terry Britten
Bass: —
Drums: Trevor Spencer

Producer: Bruce Welch
Engineer: Tony Clark
Session hours: —

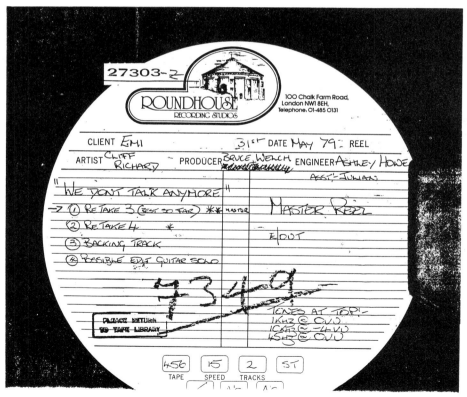

Tape box showing work carried out on *We Don't Talk Anymore*.

Studio session for EMI
26 October 1979
Abbey Road

—   Moving In   B-side

Guitar: Mart Jenner
Keyboards: Graham Todd
Drums: Clem Cattini
—: Adrian Lee
—: George Ford

Producer: Cliff Richard
Engineer: —
Recorded in studio 3
Session hours: 10.00 am–10.00 pm

Studio session for EMI
March 1980
Los Angeles

—   Suddenly   A-side

Vocals: Cliff / Olivia Newton-John

Producer: John Farrar
Engineer: —
Session hours: —

Studio sessions for EMI
5 May–13 June 1980
Riverside Studios

—   Take Another Look   I'm No
                                      Hero

—   Anything I Can Do   I'm No
                                      Hero
—   A Little In Love   A-side
—   Here (So Doggone Blue)   I'm No
                                      Hero
—   Give A Little Bit More   I'm No
                                      Hero
—   In The Night   I'm No
                                      Hero
—   I'm No Hero   I'm No
                                      Hero
—   Dreamin'   A-side
—   A Heart Will Break   I'm No
                                      Hero
—   Everyman   I'm No
                                      Hero
—   Dynamite   B-side
—   Hold On   B-side

Producer: Alan Tarney
Engineer: —
Session hours: —

Studio session for EMI
8 July 1980
Riverside Studios

—   Keep On Looking   B-side

Producer: —
Engineer: —
Session hours: —

10

Wired For Sound

1981–1983

The Records

A Little In Love / Keep On Looking	Single	15 /—
Wired For Sound / Hold On	Single	4 /—
Daddy's Home / Shakin' All Over	Single	2 /—
The Only Way Out / Under The Influence	Single	10 /—
Where Do We Go From Here / Discovering	Single	60 /—
Little Town / Love And A Helping Hand	Single	11 /—
She Means Nothing To Me / Man And A Woman	Single	9 /—
True Love Ways / Galadriel	Single	8 /—
Drifting / It's Lonely When The Lights Go Out	Single	64 /—
Never Say Die / Lucille	Single	15 /—
Please Don't Fall In Love / Too Close To Heaven	Single	7 /—
Love Songs	LP	1
Wired For Sound	LP	4
Now You See Me, Now You Don't	LP	4
Dressed For The Occasion	LP	7
Silver	LP	7

The singles released in 1981 were obvious choices for release. The live single *Daddy's Home* became the biggest hit of the year reaching the number 2 spot, and was a cover of an original by Shep and the Limelights featured on Cliff's jukebox at his home. The next single *The Only Way Out*, released in 1982, only peaked at number 10 in spite of the heavy airplay it was guaranteed as a follow-up to *Daddy's Home*. Of the next two singles, *Where Do We Go From Here* failed to appeal to a mass

audience, although the next one, *Little Town*, became a Christmas hit just outside the top ten. The first single of 1983, *She Means Nothing To Me*, was a breathtaking rock performance with Phil Everly that caught the listener's imagination and eventually peaked at number 9. The track had a lot of people sit up straight expecting more of the same. Unfortunately for those people, the next single was a ballad, but a superior one from the catalogue of Buddy Holly. *True Love Ways* did even better than the previous single, reaching number 8. Another three singles followed; of these *Never Say Die* and *Please Don't Fall In Love* were the hits.

Judged by the chart placings, this period album-wise was very successful for Cliff and EMI. However, a substantial part of the sales were taken up by the 1981 TV advertised

Publicity shot from 1981 for the *Daddy's Home* video. Cliff's brief was to look unshaven and wear a white T-shirt.

compilation album LOVE SONGS that featured all previously released material. Coming hot on the heels of this one, WIRED FOR SOUND stormed up the charts to reach the number 4 spot and had a top five single to spur interest.

Like its predecessor NOW YOU SEE ME, NOW YOU DON'T reached the same position on the album chart the following year, and did slightly better than the DRESSED FOR THE OCCASION and SILVER albums in 1983.

The Sessions

Live recordings for EMI: Hammersmith Odeon
Studio sessions for EMI: Gallery Studios
Studio sessions for EMI: Abbey Road
Studio sessions for EMI: Strawberry Studios
Live recordings for EMI: Royal Albert Hall
Studio sessions for EMI: Air Studios
Studio sessions for EMI: Mayfair Studios

For 1981 plans had been made to shoot a four-part documentary television series. The project was given the working (and final) title of "Cliff".

For inclusion the BBC simultaneously filmed and taped a concert at the Hammersmith Odeon. Cliff had some new songs in his repertoire, and of these *Daddy's Home* and *Shakin' All Over* were licensed for record release. As the BBC live recordings had not produced enough worthwhile material apart from *Daddy's Home*, more recording dates were planned for the end of May, and ran through to July. These sessions, done at Gallery Studios, produced a total of ten tracks, all for the WIRED

Recording *She Means Nothing To Me* duet with Phil Everly at Eden Studios 1982.

FOR SOUND album. Alan Tarney took over as producer, becoming responsible for all the technical and instrumental backing work. Since Alan had worked as a musician during Cliff's recent recording sessions and had witnessed his work at some of the peak periods of his career, he was only too aware of Cliff's unique talent and what was necessary to bring that talent out to the full. In this respect the partnership of Cliff and Alan was ideal. While Alan's backing work was proficient enough, the sessions still featured a number of musicians for additional accompaniment; these include Graham Jarvis and Trevor Spencer on drums, and John Clarke and Nick Glennie-Smith on guitar and keyboard work.

For the next sessions in September, Cliff returned to Abbey Road. From these, two tracks for the NOW YOU SEE ME, NOW YOU DON'T album were taped with the remaining tracks being put down at Strawberry Studios during sessions that ran through to January 1982. Apart from the album tracks the rest of the material recorded – all in the 'inspirational' genre – included some fine A- and B-side material. Of these, the reworking of *Little Town Of Bethlehem* as *Little Town* featured one of the most outstanding arrangements. The four unreleased tracks from these sessions are thought to be incomplete takes.

From a rock point of view, the highlight session of this period was the recording of *She Means Nothing To Me*, taped at Eden Studios in October 1982 during a Phil Everly session.

The track featured musicians that had not worked with Cliff before, people like Stuart Colman, Mickey Gee and Mark Knopfler. This was the kind of material that made Cliff, Phil and the band rock the plaster off the ceiling, and it seems a shame that the song never became a regular item in Cliff's live repertoire.

More recordings were planned for Cliff's concert at the Royal Albert Hall in November. For this engagement, the repertoire had undergone some changes to include more recent material, and of the songs performed, all but four were chosen for record release as the DRESSED FOR THE OCCASION album. For the first time, Cliff was accompanied by the London Philharmonic Orchestra, while some members of Cliff's studio band and backing vocalists helped out.

The songs Cliff was to record in the Strawberry Studios during May and June 1983 were to be included on the SILVER 25th commemorative album. However, during these sessions interest was not limited exclusively to new material, and some different approaches to classic rock 'n' roll material were tried out. Of these *Teddy Bear*, *Lucille* and a new reworked version of *Move It* were outstanding. These and seven others represented the material for the ROCK 'N' ROLL SILVER album that became the companion to SILVER, and released only as a limited edition two-album box set. Overdubbing of strings was carried out in July and August at Henry Wood Hall, with final mixing being done at Townhouse Studios in Late August.

Live recordings for EMI
May 1981
Hammersmith Odeon

—	Daddy's Home	A-side
—	Shakin' All Over	B-side

Guitar: John Clark
Bass: Mark Griffiths
Drums: Graham Jarvis
Keyboards: Graham Todd
Vocals: Tony Rivers

Producer: —
Engineers: —
Session hours: —

Studio session for EMI
27 May–9 July 1981
Gallery Studios

—	Wired For Sound	A-side
—	Once In A While	Wired For Sound
—	Better Than I Know Myself	Wired For Sound
—	Oh No, Don't Let Go	Wired For Sound
—	'Cos I Love That Rock 'n' Roll	Wired For Sound
—	Broken Doll	Wired For Sound

—	Lost In A Lonely World	Wired For Sound
—	Summer Rain	Wired For Sound
—	Young Love	Wired For Sound
—	Say You Don't Mind	Wired For Sound

All instruments: Alan Tarney except –
Guitar: John Clark (Lost In A Lonely World)
Drums: Graham Jarvis
       Trevor Spencer
Piano: Nick Glennie-Smith (Young Love)
Vocals: Cliff / Alan Tarney

Producer: Alan Tarney
Engineers: Nick Glennie-Smith / Ian Litle
Session hours: —

Studio sessions for EMI
9–11 September 1981
Abbey Road

| — | Son Of Thunder | Now You See Me, Now You Don't |
| — | *Take Me To The Leader* | *Unissued* |

Guitar: Mart Jenner
Keyboards: Craig Pruess
Drums: Trevor Spencer

Producer: —
Engineers: John Walker / Tony Richards
Recorded in studio: —
Session hours: 9: 11.00 am–9.00 pm
                  10: 11.00 am–10.30 pm

Cliff and David Bryce at the mixing desk 1981. Studio unknown.

Studio session for EMI
21/22 September 1981
Abbey Road

—	The Water Is Wide	Now You See Me, Now You Don't

Guitar: Mart Jenner
Bass: Mo Foster
Keyboards: Craig Pruess

Producer: —
Engineers: John Walker / Tony Richards
Recorded in studio: —
Session hours: —

Studio sessions for EMI
4–15 January 1982
Strawberry Studios

—	The Only Way Out	A-side
—	First Date	Now You See Me, Now You Don't
—	Thief In The Night	Now You See Me, Now You Don't
—	Where Do We Go From Here	A-side
—	Little Town	A-side
—	It Has To Be You, It Has To Be Me	Now You See Me, Now You Don't
—	Now You See Me, Now You Don't	Now You See Me, Now You Don't
—	Be In My Heart	Now You See Me, Now You Don't
—	Discovering	B-side
—	You, Me And Jesus	B-side
—	Under The Influence	B-side

—	*Closer To You*	*Unissued*
—	*Now That You Know Me*	*Unissued*
—	*Take Me Where I Wanna Go*	*Unissued*
—	*The Rock That Doesn't Roll*	*Unissued*

Guitars: Mart Jenner
       Bill Roberts
       John Clark
Bass: Mark Griffiths
      Paul Westwood
      Mo Foster
      Andy Pask
Drums: Dave Mattacks
       Graham Jarvis
Keyboards: Graham Todd
         Craig Pruess
Synthesizer: Dave Cooke
Piano: Peter Skellern
Percussion: Craig Pruess
Auto harp: Craig Pruess
Harmonium: Craig Pruess
Saxophone: Mel Collins
Violin: Paul Hart
Orchestra conducted by Martyn Ford
Backing vocals: Cliff / Mike Sammes Singers / Tony Rivers / Nigel Perrin

Producer: —
Engineer: Keith Bessey
Session hours: —

Studio session for EMI
June 1982
Abbey Road

—	Love And A Helping Hand	B-side

Producer: Craig Pruess
Engineer: Keith Bessey
Session hours: —

Studio session for Capitol
5 October 1982
Eden Studios, London

—	She Means Nothing To Me	A-side

Guitars: John David
  Mickey Gee
  Mark Knopfler
Bass: Stuart Colman
Drums: Terry Williams
Percussion: Rod Houison
Piano: Pete Wingfield
Vocals: Cliff / Phil Everly

Producer: Stuart Colman
Engineer: Rod Houison
Session hours: Late morning

Lead vocals on this track are by Phil Everly and Cliff.

Live recordings for EMI
23 November 1982
Royal Albert Hall

—	Green Light	Dressed For The Occasion
—	We Don't Talk Anymore	Dressed For The Occasion
—	True Love Ways	Dressed For The Occasion
—	Softly As I Leave You	Dressed For The Occasion
—	Carrie	Dressed For The Occasion
—	Miss You Nights	Dressed For The Occasion
—	Galadriel	Dressed For The Occasion
—	Maybe Someday	Dressed For The Occasion
—	Thief In The Night	Dressed For The Occasion
—	Up In The World	Dressed For The Occasion
—	Treasure Of Love	Dressed For The Occasion
—	Devil Woman / Reprise	Dressed For The Occasion
—	*Discovering*	*Unissued*
—	*You, Me And Jesus*	*Unissued*
—	*Daddy's Home*	*Unissued*
—	*Little Town*	*Unissued*

The London Philharmonic Orchestra conducted by Richard Hewson
Synthesizer: David Cooke
Bass: Mark Griffiths
Drums: Graham Jarvis
Piano: Steve Gray
Vocals: Tony Rivers / Tony Harding / Stuart Calver / John Perry

Producers: Cliff Richard / Richard Hewson
Engineer: John Kurlander
Session hours: —

Recorded on Pumacrest Mobile by Doug Hopkins

Mixed at Strawberry Studios South by Keith Bessey.

Studio session for DJM
Date unknown
Studio unknown

—	Driftin'	A-side

Producer: —
Engineer: —
Session hours: —

Studio sessions for EMI
7–12 March 1983
Abbey Road

—	Back In Vaudeville	Foreign B-side

Musicians: —

Producer: Bruce Welch
Engineer: —
Recorded in the Penthouse studio and others
Session hours: —

The above information was taken from session sheets logged
at EMI. No further details have come to light so it is
impossible to tell what else was recorded.

Studio sessions for EMI
21/22/23 March 1983
Air Recording Studios, London

—	Please Don't Fall In Love	A-side
—	Too Close To Heaven	B-side
—	*How To Handle A Woman*	*Unissued*

Guitars: Ray Russell
      Alan Parker
Bass: Frank McDonald
Drums: Graham Jarvis
Percussion: Ray Cooper
      Tony Carr
Keyboards: Mike Batt
Vocals: Mike Batt/Cliff
Orchestra: —

Producers: Mike Batt/Bruce Welch
Engineer: Steve Churchyard
Recorded in studio 2
Session hours: 21: 10.00 am–6.00 pm
           22: 11.00 am–2.00 pm
           23: 2.00 pm–1.30 am

Strings were recorded at C.T.S. Wembley, possibly on the
21st and engineered by Dick Lewsey.

Studio sessions for EMI
9 May–3 June/6–17, 19, 26 June 1983
Strawberry Studios South

—	Silver's Home Tonight	Silver
—	Hold On	Silver
—	Front Page	Silver
—	Ocean Deep	Silver
—	Locked Inside Your Prison	Silver
—	The Golden Days Are Over	Silver
—	Love Stealer	Silver
—	Makin' History	Rock 'n' Roll Silver
—	Move It	Rock 'n' Roll Silver
—	Donna	Rock 'n' Roll Silver
—	Teddy Bear	Rock 'n' Roll Silver
—	It'll Be Me	Rock 'n' Roll Silver
—	Lucille	Rock 'n' Roll Silver
—	Little Bitty Pretty One	Rock 'n' Roll Silver
—	Never Be Anyone Else But You	Rock 'n' Roll Silver
—	Be Bop A Lula	Rock 'n' Roll Silver
—	Tutti Frutti	Rock 'n' Roll Silver

Guitars: John Clark
      Mart Jenner
Bass: Mark Griffiths
Keyboards: Dave Cooke
         Craig Pruess
         Alan Park
Drums: Graham Jarvis
Saxophone: Mel Collins
Synthesizers: Craig Pruess
Orchestra conducted by Martyn Ford
Vocals: Cliff/Tony Rivers/Stu Calver/John
Perry

Producer: Craig Pruess
Engineer: Keith Bessey
Session hours: —

Strings were recorded at Henry Wood Hall during July/
August.

Mixed at The Townhouse Studios July/August.

Studio sessions for EMI
21/22 May 1983
Mayfair Recording Studios

| — | Never Say Die (Give A Little Bit More) | Silver |

Guitar: Terry Britten
Bass: Mark Griffiths
Drums: Graham Jarvis
Keyboards: Nick Glennie-Smith
Saxophone: Ronnie Asprey
Trumpet: Martin Drover
Vocals: Terry Britten

Producer: Terry Britten
Engineer: John Hudson
Recorded in studio 1
Session hours: 21: 10.20 am–10.30 pm
                        22: 10.30 am–9.30 pm

Overdubs and mixing were carried out on 28/29 May, 7/21 June and 22 July.

Studio session for EMI
August 1983
Abbey Road

—   Baby You're Dynamite   A-side

Guitar: Nigel Jenkins
Bass: Alan Jones
Drums: Brian Bennett
Keyboards: Guy Fletcher
Vocals: Cliff / Guy Fletcher

Producer: Bruce Welch
Engineer: Peter Vince
Recorded in studio: —
Session hours: —

11

Silver

1984–1987

The Records

Baby You're Dynamite / Ocean Deep	Single	27 / —
Two To The Power / Rock And Roll	Single	
Shooting From The Heart / Small World	Single	51 / —
Heart User / I Will Follow You	Single	46 / —
She's So Beautiful / She's So Beautiful	Single	17 / —
It's In Every One Of Us / Alone	Single	45 / —
Living Doll / Happy	Single	1 / —
Born To Rock 'n' Roll / Law Of The Universe	Single	
All I Ask Of You / Overture	Single	3 / —
Slow Rivers / Billy And The Kids	Single	44 / —
My Pretty One / Love Ya	Single	6 / —
Some People / One Time Lover Man	Single	3 / —
Remember Me / Another Christmas Day	Single	35 / —
The Rock Connection	LP	43
Always Guaranteed	LP	5

Given the quality of the three singles released, 1984 surprisingly turned out to be a very poor year for Cliff on the singles chart. The duet with Janet Jackson on *Two To The Power* definitely showed promise, but the single failed to register at all, and although neither of the other two singles were big hits, they still did considerably better than this one. While suffering from the same defect, two of the singles released the following year just did not have enough impact to score big on the charts. However, the public was not slow to pick up on *She's So Beautiful* sending this, the first single from "Time – The Musical", to a top twenty position and staying on the chart for nine weeks. Two of the four singles in 1986 reached the top three. Of these the new comic version of *Living Doll* with The Young Ones repeated its 1959 success of reaching the pinnacle of the charts, while *All I Ask Of You*, duetted with Sarah Brightman, peaked at number 3. Another duet, this time with Elton John on *Slow Rivers*, did not do as well. Two tracks, *My Pretty One* and *Some People*, culled from the ALWAYS GUARANTEED album were selected for single release and became Cliff's two top ten hits in a row for 1987. Even though one more single was lifted from the album, *Remember Me* failed to repeat the success of the previous two, only achieving moderate success at number 35.

The same fate befell the 1984 album THE ROCK CONNECTION, and despite containing some fine newly recorded material, the album consisted of mainly previously released tracks from ROCK 'N' ROLL SILVER, and consequently sales and chart action were disappointing, but perhaps the album was only released as EMI may have been impatient to get new product out.

However, ALWAYS GUARANTEED released in September 1987 became Cliff's most successful studio album.

The Sessions

Studio session for A & M: Advision
Studio session for Rocket: SOL Studios
Studio sessions for EMI: Gallery Studios
Studio sessions for EMI: Strawberry Studios
Studio sessions for EMI: Roundhouse Studios
Studio session for EMI: Marcus Studio
Studio session for WEA: Master Rock Studios
Studio session for EMI: Abbey Road

The material recorded at the first two sessions of this period was in the duet category. *Two To*

The Power was taped at Advision studios with Janet Jackson, and *Slow Rivers* with Elton John was done at SOL studios during the recording of his FIRE ON ICE album.

Although the June/July sessions belong to material that started out as a TV project, only six new recordings were put on tape. Of these the reworking of *Willie And The Hand Jive* is an outstanding arrangement of the 1959 hit, and of the new material *Heart User* is instilled with all the fire and electricity of a fifties

1986 COPYRIGHT EMI RECORDS (UK) - PHOTOGRAPHER: FRANK GRIFFIN

T I M E
THE MUSICAL

performance. Producer credits were shared between Cliff and engineer Keith Bessey, and in the same vein as ROCK 'N' ROLL SILVER, the band was trimmed down to a basic rock line-up. However, as these sessions had not produced enough material for an album, it was decided to add the Phil Everly duet remixed, together with *Dynamite* and a further six songs from ROCK 'N' ROLL SILVER for release as THE ROCK CONNECTION.

No studio sessions took place again until December when in preparation for his leading role in the West End Musical "Time" plans were put into action for Cliff to record at the Roundhouse studios where he put down the vocals to *She's So Beautiful*. Stevie Wonder produced, arranged and played on the track that became the first featured single. Material recorded during the next sessions in June and August were also tied in to the musical and provided another two A-sides.

The first sessions for 1986 took place in January at the Master Rock studios with Stuart Colman producing a special remake of Cliff's 1959 hit *Living Doll* for Comic Relief. Vocals for the track were laid down by Cliff and the alternative comedy team of The Young Ones in

only 20 minutes, although mixing took up to six weeks. Of the musicians for this session, there was a change personnel-wise, but only on this occasion – Tim Renwick on guitar, Howard Tibble on drums, Stuart Colman on bass and Pete Wingfield on keyboard. Of the old Shadows crew, Hank Marvin was in the studio to recreate his original 1959 guitar solo.

Because of Cliff's total involvement with "Time", recording sessions over this period became correspondingly more difficult to schedule. However, afternoon sessions at RG Jones Studios running from September produced all the tracks for the ALWAYS GUARANTEED album as well as some B-sides. Alan Tarney provided the technical and musical expertise by playing all instrumentation on the backing tracks as well as supervising production of the sessions. One new talent brought in for the recording of *Under Your Spell* was Chris Eaton who helped out on additional keyboard work, but only on this track.

In addition, a session in August took Cliff back to Abbey Road to duet with Sarah Brightman on *All I Ask Of You* with Andrew Lloyd Webber producing.

Studio session for A & M
26 April 1984
Advision

—	Two To The Power	A-side

Producer: —
Engineer: —
Session hours: 7.00 pm–10.00 pm

This track is a duet with Janet Jackson.

Studio session for Rocket
15 May 1984
The SOL Studios

—	Slow Rivers	A-side

Piano: Elton John
Guitar: Davey Johnstone
Bass: David Paton
Keyboards: Fred Mandell
Drums: Dave Mattacks

Producer: Gus Dudgeon
Engineer: —
Session hours: 8.00 pm–10.00 pm

This is a duet with Elton John.

The musicians on this track are probably the same as those featured on Elton John's Fire On Ice album.

Studio session for EMI
24 June 1984
Gallery Studios

—	La Gonave	The Rock Connection
—	Small World	B-side
—	I Will Follow You	B-side
—	*Tiny Planet*	*Unissued*

Producers: Cliff Richard / Craig Pruess
Engineer: Keith Bessey
Session hours: —

**Studio sessions for EMI
23–28 July 1984
Strawberry Studios South**

—	Learning How To Rock 'n' Roll	The Rock Connection
—	Heart User	The Rock Connection
—	Willie And The Hand Jive	The Rock Connection
—	Lovers And Friends	The Rock Connection
—	Over You	The Rock Connection
—	Shooting From The Heart	The Rock Connection

Producers: Cliff Richard / Keith Bessey
Engineer: Keith Bessey
Session hours: —

**Studio session for EMI
20/21 December 1984
Roundhouse Studios**

— She's So Beautiful   A-side

All instruments played by Stevie Wonder and recorded at Wonderland Studios, Los Angeles.

Producer: Stevie Wonder
Engineer: —
Session hours: —

**Studio session for EMI
10/11 June 1985
Gallery Studios**

— It's In Every One Of Us   A-side

Guitar: John Clark
Bass: Andy Pask
Drums: Graham Jarvis
Keyboards: Craig Pruess
Strings: Martin Loveday / Gavyn Wright

Producers: Keith Bessey / Craig Pruess
Engineer: Keith Bessey
Session hours: —

**Studio session for EMI
25 August 1985
Marcus Studios London**

— Born To Rock 'n' Roll   A-side

Guitar: Billy Squire
Bass: Jerry Hay
Drums: Graham Jarvis
Keyboards: Dave Stewart
Vocals: Billy Squire

Producer: Peter Collins
Engineer: Chris Porter
Session hours: —

Mixed at Sarm between 29 August and 2 September.

**Studio session for WEA
29 January 1986
Master Rock Studios**

— Living Doll   A-side

Guitars: Hank Marvin
       Tim Renwick
Bass: Stuart Colman
Drums: Howard Tibble
Keyboards: Peter Wingfield
Vocals: Cliff / Nigel Planer / Rik Mayall / Adrian Edmondson / Christopher Ryan

Producer: Stuart Colman
Engineers: Carb Kanelle / Damien Asker-Brown
Session hours: 7.00 pm–10.00 pm

**Studio session for Polydor
6 August 1986
Abbey Road**

— All I Ask Of You   A-side

Vocals: Cliff / Sarah Brightman

Producer: Andrew Lloyd Webber
Engineer: —
Session hours: —

Interior of control room at RG Jones Studios in Wimbledon. (Photo taken in 1990).

Studio sessions for EMI
September 1986
RG Jones

—	One Night	Always Guaranteed
—	Once Upon A Time	Always Guaranteed
—	Some People	A-side
—	Forever	Always Guaranteed
—	Two Hearts	Always Guaranteed
—	Under Your Spell	Always Guaranteed
—	This Time Now	Always Guaranteed
—	My Pretty One	A-side
—	Remember Me	A-side
—	Always Guaranteed	Always Guaranteed

—	Love Ya	B-side
—	Under The Gun	B-side
—	One Time Lover Man	B-side
—	Another Christmas Day	B-side
—	Yesterday, Today, Forever	B-side
—	Wild Geese	B-side

Guitars / Bass / Keyboards / Programming: Alan Tarney
Additional keyboards: Chris Eaton

Producer: Alan Tarney
Engineers: Gerry Kitchingham / Keith Bessey
Session hours: —

12

Always Guaranteed

1988–1990

The Records

Two Hearts /		
Yesterday, Today, Forever	Single	34 / —
Mistletoe And Wine / Marmaduke	Single	1 / —
The Best Of Me / Move It	Single	2 / —
Just Don't Have The Heart /		
Wide Open Space	Single	3 / —
Lean On You / Hey Mister	Single	17 / —
Stronger Than That / Joanna	Single	14 / —
Silhouettes / The Winner	Single	10 / —
From A Distance /		
Lindsay Jane II	Single	11 / —
Saviour's Day /		
The "Oh Boy" Medley	Single	1 / —
Private Collection 1979–1988	LP	1
Stronger	LP	7
The EP Collection	LP	
From A Distance – The Event	LP	3

This period was to become one of the most successful for Cliff. Of the two singles released in 1988 *Mistletoe And Wine* became a massive Christmas hit and the biggest selling single of that year, staying in the number 1 spot over the festive season. The follow-up single was the beautiful ballad *The Best Of Me*, making Cliff the first British artist to release 100 singles and it occupied the number 2 spot on the singles chart in the spring of 1989. The third top three single in a row was with *Just Don't Have The Heart* produced by hitmakers Stock, Aitken and Waterman, and although neither of the last two singles of the year were big hits they still managed top twenty positions. Given the quality and excellent choice of singles released in 1990, it seems incredible that *Silhouettes* and *From A Distance* didn't reach any higher on the charts than the number 10 and 11 positions respectively. Of course the Christmas single *Saviour's Day* was the biggest seller of the year, repeating the success of *Mistletoe And Wine*.

Sales of the albums during this period reached to the level of the singles. PRIVATE COLLECTION featured the very best recordings from 1979–1988, occupying the number 1 spot on the album chart as Cliff's 30th year ended. Although the next one, STRONGER, was released to jubilant reviews, perhaps it lost out somewhat to the fact that four hit singles were culled from the album. Of course, the FROM A DISTANCE – THE EVENT double album resulted in exceptional sales figures largely due to the memento aspect of Cliff's two great evenings at Wembley Stadium – not only for those who were there, but for those who weren't and realised what they had missed.

The Sessions

Studio sessions for EMI: RG Jones
Studio sessions for EMI: Battery Studios
Studio sessions for EMI: PWL Studios

Live recordings for EMI: Wembley Stadium
Studio sessions for EMI: JFM Studios
Live recordings for Polydor: Knebworth

Typical EMI campaign dealer ad in 'Music Week'.

The June 1988 sessions at RG Jones were set up to record the *Mistletoe And Wine* Christmas single with two days of additional recording held in July. A third series of sessions was held in August to produce a new B-side and the first material for the STRONGER album. *Share A Dream* featured Aswad playing all the instruments and providing backing vocals as well as producing the track.

Cliff's vocal for *Just Don't Have The Heart*, the dance track produced by Stock, Aitken and Waterman, was done at the PWL studio from 23 January to 13 February, although mixing and re-mixing sessions continued through to August when backing vocals and additional accompaniment were added to the basic rhythm track. A definite disadvantage of this procedure was Cliff's absence when this work was done, as final mixes would be submitted to Cliff and he would perhaps occasionally ask for certain changes to be made.

The sessions running through to May at RG Jones were taken up with more and final work for the STRONGER album. The band and back-up singers consisted mainly of the regular members of Cliff's live band, although additional backing vocals were done by Cliff and Alan Tarney. The repertoire still represented good quality material, making the results of these sessions outstanding. Recordings like *Stronger Than That*, *The Best Of Me*, *Lean On You* and *Joanna*, though perhaps not being sensational, made great music indeed.

The Stones Mobile Recording Unit was

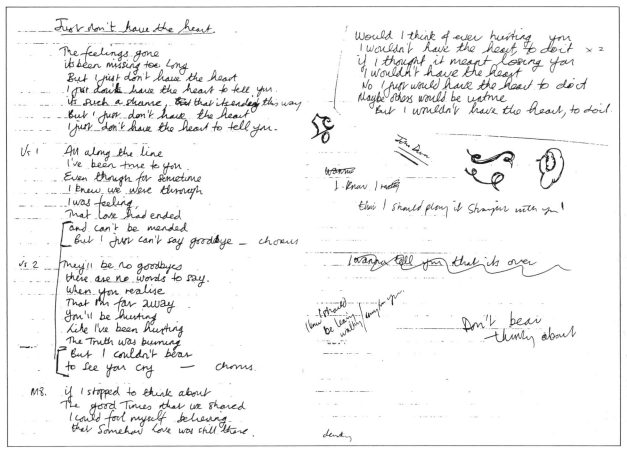

Example of rough stages for lyrics of *Just Don't Have The Heart*.

installed in the grounds at Wembley Stadium to record the "Event" concerts on 16 and 17 June. Engineered by Mick McKenna and Keith Bessey both shows were taped in their entirety providing an enormous amount of material to select from for the FROM A DISTANCE – THE EVENT album. In this respect some crucial decisions had to be made of the tracks to include and of those to be omitted. For the five and a half hour shows, Cliff worked with the original Oh Boy! team of the Dallas Boys and the Vernon Girls, was reunited with the Shadows, duetted with Aswad and the Kalin Twins, and rocked with Jet Harris and Tony Meehan, as well as being backed by his regular live band on his own set. Mixing of tracks for the album took place at RG Jones, Sarm West and PWL.

The next studio sessions took place in December with Cliff visiting the PWL studios again, this time to take part in the recording of *Do They Know It's Christmas* for Band Aid II, a project designed to raise money for famine in Ethiopia. The track, produced by Stock, Aitken and Waterman, was taped over two days on the 3rd and 4th with Cliff and other artists contributing vocals.

More live recordings were done in June 1990 at the concert in aid of the Nordoff-Robbins Music Therapy Centre. Cliff was again reunited with the Shadows for a 45 minute set, and although broadcast live in its entirety on Radio One, only *On The Beach* and *Do You Wanna Dance* were used on KNEBWORTH – THE ALBUM. There was no time for repair work to be done as it was planned to have the album in the shops right on the heels of all the media hullabaloo.

Cliff returned to RG Jones for his only other studio sessions for 1990. These provided a new B-side for *From A Distance* and the song Cliff had selected for his Christmas single. *Saviour's Day* was laid down in three days during July

1989 / 23613
© EMI RECORDS (UK) · PHOTOGRAPHER: PETER VERNON
CLIFF RICHARD

with guitar overdubs by John Clark being added on the 20th and vocal backings on the 21st. With Cliff producing, final mixing of the tracks was done over two days assisted by Gerry Kitchingham, Paul Moessl and Ben Robbins.

The authors were given the privilege to observe Cliff recording *Saviour's Day* and will look back on this and all the great recording work done by him over the years with a total commitment to his public and to his fans. Whether work took place in London, Paris, Barcelona, New York or Nashville, Cliff always gave his very best so as not to short-change his fans. Any fan or record enthusiast in thinking of the body of Cliff's recorded work can rest assured of the place the songs and the man have claimed for themselves, and know that in the future no discussion of twentieth-century popular music can take place without the mention of Cliff Richard.

Studio sessions for EMI
6–10 June and 12–13 July 1988
RG Jones

—   Mistletoe And Wine   A-side

Keyboards/Synthesizers/Drum programming:
Paul Moessl
Bass: Mark Griffiths
Strings arranged and conducted by Paul Moessl.

Producer: Cliff Richard
Engineer: —
Session hours: —

Strings were probably overdubbed during the July sessions.

Studio session for EMI
August 1988
RG Jones

—   All The Time You Need   B-side
—   Marmaduke   B-side

Guitars: John Clark
             Steve Lauri
Bass: Mark Griffiths
Drums: Henry Spinetti
Piano: Alan Parks
Synthesizers: Paul Moessl
Vocals: Micky Mullins/Peter Howarth/Keith Murrell

Producer: —
Engineer: Gerry Kitchingham
Session hours: —

Studio sessions for EMI
29–31 August 1988
Battery Studios

—   Share A Dream   Stronger

All instruments and backing vocals: Aswad

Producers: Aswad
Engineer: Godwin Logie
Recorded in 'The Lighthouse' studio
Session hours: —

Studio sessions for EMI
20 January–7 August 1989
PWL Studios

—   Just Don't Have The Heart   A-side

Keyboards: Mike Stock
                Matt Aitken
Drums: A. Linn
Vocals: Mae McKenna/Miriam Stockley

Producers: Stock/Aitken/Waterman
Engineers: Karen Hewitt/Yoyo
Recorded in studios 1 and 2
Session hours: —

The dates listed above are not only for recording but include writing, recording, mixing and re-mixing.

According to the session sheets the track was recorded between 23 January and 13 February.

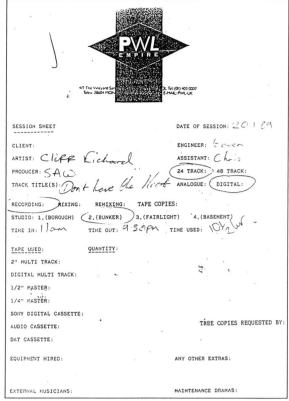

Detailed session sheet from PWL's official files.

Detailed remix sheet for *Stranger Than That* from the files of Mayfair Recording Studios.

Studio sessions for EMI
March/20-22 April/6 May 1989
RG Jones

—	Stronger Than That	A-side
—	Who's In Love	Stronger
—	The Best Of Me	A-side
—	Clear Blue Skies	Stronger
—	Lean On You	A-side
—	Keep Me Warm	Stronger
—	Joanna	B-side
—	Everybody Knows	Stronger
—	Forever You Will Be Mine	Stronger
—	Better Day	Stronger
—	Wide Open Space	B-side
—	Hey Mister	B-side
—	Lindsay Jane	B-side

—: Alan Tarney
Guitar: John Clark
Bass: Mark Griffiths
Drum programming: Keith Bessey

Saxophone: Dave Bishop
Vocals: Cliff/Alan Tarney/Mick Mullins/Keith Murrell

Producers: Alan Tarney/Cliff Richard
Engineers: Gerry Kitchingham/Ben Robbins
Session hours: —

Live recordings for EMI
16/17 June 1989
Wembley Stadium

—	Oh Boy Medley	
—	Whole Lotta Shakin' Goin' On	From A Distance
—	Bird Dog	From A Distance
—	Let's Have A Party	From A Distance

EMI campaign dealer ad for FROM A DISTANCE – THE EVENT in 'Music Week' November 1990.

—	It's My Party	From A Distance
—	C'Mon Everybody	From A Distance
—	Whole Lotta Shakin' Goin' On	From A Distance
—	Zing Went The Strings Of My Heart	From A Distance
—	Always	From A Distance
—	When	From A Distance
—	The Glory Of Love	From A Distance
—	Hoots Mon	From A Distance
—	Don't Look Now	From A Distance
—	The Girl Can't Help It	From A Distance
—	Sea Cruise	From A Distance
—	Medley:	
—	Book Of Love	From A Distance
—	Blue Moon	From A Distance
—	Do You Wanna Dance	From A Distance
—	Chantilly Lace	From A Distance
—	At The Hop	From A Distance
—	Rock 'n' Roll Is Here To Stay	From A Distance

The Oh Boy Band

—	The Young Ones	From A Distance
—	In The Country	From A Distance
—	*Bachelor Boy*	*Unissued*
—	*Willie And The Hand Jive*	*Unissued*
—	*Living Doll*	*Unissued*
—	*Please Don't Tease*	*Unissued*
—	*Dynamite*	*Unissued*
—	*It'll Be Me*	*Unissued*

Guitars: Hank Marvin
      Bruce Welch
Bass: Mark Griffiths
Drums: Brian Bennett
Keyboards: Cliff Hall
Saxophone: Ray Beavis

—	Wired For Sound	B-side
—	*Dreamin'*	*Unissued*
—	*Daddy's Home*	*Unissued*
—	I Could Easily Fall In Love	B-side
—	Some People	From A Distance
—	We Don't Talk Anymore	From A Distance
—	*Two Hearts*	*Unissued*
—	Move It	From A Distance
—	Shake, Rattle And Roll	From A Distance
—	*Joanna*	*Unissued*
—	*Remember Me*	*Unissued*
—	*Stronger Than That*	*Unissued*
—	Silhouettes	A-side
—	Good Golly Miss Molly	From A Distance
—	*Miss You Nights*	*Unissued*
—	Summer Holiday	From A Distance
—	*Just Don't Have The Heart*	*Unissued*
—	God Put A Fighter In Me	From A Distance
—	Thief In The Night	From A Distance
—	*The Best Of Me*	*Unissued*
—	From A Distance	A-side

Guitars: John Clark
      Steve Lauri
Bass: Steve Stroud
Drums: Peter May
Keyboards: Alan Park
      Paul Moessl
Guitar: Jet Harris
Drums: Tony Meehan
Vocals: Mick Mullins / Peter Howarth / Keith Murrell / Sonia Morgan / Tessa Niles

Producer: —
Engineers: Keith Bessey / Mick McKenna
Session hours: —

Mixed at Sarm during late 1989 and early 1990.

H2.

SARM

SARM STUDIOS (WEST)   8/10 BASING STREET   LONDON W11 1ET   TELEPHONE: 01-229 1229   TELEX 297314

ARTIST	CLIENT	STUDIO	DATE	DISKETTE No.
CLIFF RICHARD	CRO	ONE	30.6.90	

PRODUCER	ENGINEER	ASSISTANT DANTON
KEITH BESSEY	KEITH	COPY ENGINEER

TITLE	TAKE	TIME	SPIRAL	TITLE	TAKE	SPIRAL
"YOUNG ONES"			FILL	MASTER.		
'IN THE COUNTRY'			PTEL	MASTER		
'SHARE A DREAM"			FTEL	MASTER -		

REMARKS TONTES ON REEL H1

TOTAL RUNNING TIME: _____

DOLBY TONE @	MARK	LEVEL	Hz@	VU	HIGH	Khz@	VU	LOW	Hz@	VU
☐48 TRACK ☐24 TRACK ☐16 TRACK		☐ MASTER	☐ SLAVE		◩ STEREO	☐ MONO		No.	OF	REELS

Tape box for some of the recordings from the EVENT concerts at Wembley Stadium June 1989.

Studio session for EMI
September 1989
JFM Studios Twickenham

—   Where You Are   B-side

Producer: Dave Cooke
Engineer: —
Session hours: —

Studio sessions for Polydor
3/4 December 1989
PWL Studios

—   Do They Know It's Christmas A-side

Keyboards: Mike Stock
                Matt Aitken
Guitars: Matt Aitken
             Chris Rea
Drums: A. Linn
             Luke Goss

Recording *Saviour's Day* at RG Jones Studios in Wimbledon July 1990.

Producers: Stock / Aitken / Waterman
Engineers: Karen Hewitt / Yoyo
Recorded in studios 1 and 4
Session hours: 3: 10.00 am–2.00 pm
4: 11.00 am–8.30 pm

Cliff features on this track with Bananarama / Big Fun / Bros /
Cathy Dennis / DMob / Jason Donovan / Kevin Godley / Glen
Goldsmith / Kylie Minogue / The Pasadenas / Chris Rea /
Jimmy Sommerville / Sonia / Lisa Stansfield / Technotronics /
Wet Wet Wet.

Studio session for EMI
December 1989
JFM Studios Twickenham

—	The Winner	B-side

Producer: Dave Cooke
Engineer: —
Session hours: —

Live recordings for Polydor
30 June 1990
Knebworth

—	*Move It*	*Unissued*
—	*Summer Holiday*	*Unissued*
—	*The Young Ones*	*Unissued*
—	On The Beach	Knebworth – The Album
—	*Living Doll*	*Unissued*
—	*Good Golly Miss Molly*	*Unissued*
—	*Bachelor Boy*	*Unissued*
—	*I Could Easily Fall (In Love With You)*	*Unissued*
—	Do You Wanna Dance	Knebworth – The Album
—	*In The Country*	*Unissued*
—	*It'll Be Me*	*Unissued*
—	*Shake, Rattle And Roll*	*Unissued*
—	*We Don't Talk Anymore*	*Unissued*

Guitars: Hank Marvin
Bruce Welch

Bass: Mark Griffiths
Drums: Brian Bennett
Keyboards: Cliff Hall
Synthesizers: Paul Moessl
Brass: Ray Beavis / Dick Hanson / Chris Gower /
John Earle
Vocals: Hank Marvin / Bruce Welch / Mick
Mullins / Pete Howarth / Keith Murrell

Producer: —
Engineers: —
Session hours: 3.30 pm–4.15 pm

The entire show was broadcast 'live' on BBC Radio One but
only two tracks were used on KNEBWORTH – THE ALBUM.

Studio sessions for EMI
16–24 July 1990
RG Jones

—	Lindsay Jane II	B-side
—	Saviour's Day	A-side

Guitar: John Clark
Keyboards / Synthesizers / Drum programming:
Paul Moessl
Vocals: Cliff / Pete Howarth / Keith Murrell /
Miriam Stockley / Mae McKenna

Producer: Cliff Richard
Engineers: Gerry Kitchingham / Paul Moessl /
Ben Robbins
Session hours: —

Recording Technology

One who has had the privilege to witness Cliff Richard at work on a recording session will recognise a true professional in action. From the day he first set foot into Abbey Road way back in 1958 it was immediately obvious that his microphone technique and sense of timing were superb. The fact that he has retained everlasting youth in a very fast-moving technological environment has much to do with his ability not only to understand these rapid changes but also to converse in the vocabulary that has grown up within the world of recording studios.

One of the major developments in recording had taken place only a few years before Cliff arrived on the scene. Round about 1950 the tape machine began to replace the long-standing method of cutting directly onto wax. The introduction of magnetic tape opened up a series of new possibilities. In the days of wax each cut was live and mistakes could only be rectified by recording the entire programme again. Tape allied to a pair of non-magnetic scissors or a razor blade enabled different tapes to be edited or spliced together to form a master. By using two tape machines one could add the original with new sounds from the studio, both recorded onto the second tape machine, a process originally referred to as superimposition. This method, however, added noise and distortion but the technique was to be the forerunner for multi-track machines which came into prominence in the sixties. Whereas 3-track machines were to be adopted in the USA, the UK and Europe adopted the 4-track machine. It was a Studer J37 that was the base for experiments at Abbey Road in the mid-sixties. The beauty of this machine was the fact that the record head also doubled as a replay head and a signal could be sent from this output

to an artist in the studio who would then record onto a hitherto unused track. In this way a recording could be built up in a similar way as an artist paints a picture on canvas. 4-track had its obvious limitations and about every four years further developments took place, firstly to 8-track, then to 16, on to 24, and finally locking two 24s together in synchronisation, giving 48-track.

It was not only tape machines but all other items of electronic equipment which were being subjected to rapid change. Mixing consoles like tape machines had originally been home-made by the research and development sections of major record companies, who also owned studios. As the number of studios expanded and many became independent, so these items began to be manufactured by specialist companies such as Rupert Neve and later by Solid State Logic, and they also became bigger and bigger, to incorporate all the latest requirements. Outboard equipment, commonly known as toys, such as limiters, compressors, expanders, noise gates, echo and double-tracking devices, became musts for every self-respecting studio.

Having built up a multi-track tape, mixing it down originally to mono and later stereo, and for a short while quadrophonic, became a very important function. As time moved on so this process changed from a manual operation to one which used computers, such as the SSL total recall.

The weak link in the recording chain remained the analogue tape machine, which had an inferior signal-to-noise ratio compared to the rest of the equipment. This was originally improved by Dolby noise reduction, and recently by a more powerful system known as

SR, but it was this original weakness that led to developments of digital tape machines. Initially stereo and later multi-track machines benefited by the signal being converted to numbers, with a greatly enhanced performance and the ability to copy indefinitely without any degradation whatsoever. Around this new technology have developed hard disc stores and a tremendous range of electronic devices using signal processing for both the control room and the studio. The technology, too, has changed for the general public, with the advent of compact disc enabling the quality at home to match the quality in the studio.

Cliff Richard has been at the forefront of all these changes in technology and has continued to make hit records using all the various formats. Throughout all this time he has remained one of the greatest ambassadors the pop recording industry has ever known.

Ken Townsend
Director of Operations
Abbey Road Studios

Recording–Technical Terminology

Acetate   A disc cut for evaluation purposes only, and often taken away by the artist.

Backing tracks   Pre-recorded tape on which an artist will overdub his vocals and/or other instruments.

Demo   Disc usually used for artistic evaluation.

Edit (piece)   Section of tape spliced in to improve or replace an existing piece.

8-track tape   Tape with eight separate tracks for recording.

Fade in   Raising a signal to an audible level.

Fade out   Reduction of a signal to an inaudible level, often used at the close of a song.

False start   An incomplete take, often caused by the artist or musician singing or playing a wrong note.

4-track tape   Tape with four separate tracks for recording.

Master   Version finally chosen for release.

Mono remix   Remix down from multiple track to a single track.

Out-take   Other versions of a song, not used as the master.

Overdubs   Process of adding extra vocals / instruments to an already existing track.

Reduction   Mixing together existing tracks and transferring them onto fewer tracks on another tape.

Rill   Gap inserted between two tracks, normally silent.

16-track tape   Tape with sixteen separate tracks for recording.

Splice   *See* Edit.

Stereo remix   Remix down from multiple track to a stereo (2-track) master.

Superimposition   *See* Overdubs.

Tape-to-tape   Transfer from one tape machine to another.

32-track tape   Tape with 32 separate tracks for recording.

2-track tape   Tape with two separate tracks for recording.

Complete UK Discography
1958–1990

Singles

Move It / Schoolboy Crush
DB 4178
August 1958

High Class Baby / My Feet Hit The Ground
DB 4203
November 1958

Livin' Lovin' Doll / Steady With You
DB 4249
January 1959

Mean Streak / Never Mind
DB 4290
April 1959

Living Doll / Apron Strings
DB 4306
July 1959

Travellin' Light / Dynamite
DB 4351
October 1959

A Voice In The Wilderness /
   Don't Be Mad At Me
DB 4398
January 1960

Fall In Love With You /
   Willie And The Hand Jive
DB 4431
March 1960

Please Don't Tease / Where Is My Heart?
DB 4479
June 1960

Nine Times Out Of Ten /
   Thinking Of Our Love
DB 4506
September 1960

I Love You / 'D' In Love
DB 4547
November 1960

Theme For A Dream / Mumblin' Mosie
DB 4593
February 1961

Gee Whiz It's You /
   I Cannot Find A True Love
DC 756
March 1961

A Girl Like You /
   Now's The Time To Fall In Love
DB 4667
June 1961

When The Girl In Your Arms (Is The Girl In
   Your Heart) / Got A Funny Feeling
DB 4716
October 1961

What'd I Say / Blue Moon
DC 758
1961

The Young Ones / We Say Yeah
DB 4761
January 1962

**I'm Looking Out The Window /
   Do You Wanna Dance**
DB 4828
May 1962

It'll Be Me / Since I Lost You
DB 4886
August 1962

The Next Time / Bachelor Boy
DB 4950
November 1962

Summer Holiday / Dancing Shoes
DB 4977
February 1963

Lucky Lips / I Wonder
DB 7034
May 1963

**It's All In The Game /
   Your Eyes Tell On You**
DB 7089
August 1963

Don't Talk To Him / Say You're Mine
DB 7150
November 1963

**I'm The Lonely One /
   Watch What You Do With My Baby**
DB 7203
January 1964

Constantly / True, True Lovin'
DB 7272
April 1964

On The Beach / A Matter Of Moments
DB 7305
June 1964

**The Twelfth Of Never /
   I'm Afraid To Go Home**
DB 7372
October 1964

**I Could Easily Fall (In Love With You) /
   I'm In Love With You**
DB 7420
December 1964

**This Was My Special Day /
   I'm Feeling Oh So Lonely**
DB 7435
December 1964

The Minute You're Gone / Just Another Guy
DB 7496
March 1965

Angel / Razzle Dazzle
DC 762
May 1965

On My Word / Just A Little Bit Too Late
DB 7596
June 1965

**The Time In Between /
   Look Before You Love**
DB 7660
August 1965

Wind Me Up / The Night
DB 7745
October 1965

Blue Turns To Grey / Somebody Loses
DB 7866
March 1966

**Visions / What Would I Do (For The Love Of
   A Girl)**
DB 7968
July 1966

Time Drags By / The La La La Song
DB 8017
October 1966

In The Country / Finders Keepers
DB 8094
December 1966

It's All Over / Why Wasn't I Born Rich?
DB 8150
March 1967

I'll Come Running / I Got The Feelin'
DB 8210
June 1967

The Day I Met Marie / Our Story Book
DB 8245
August 1967

All My Love / Sweet Little Jesus Boy
DB 8293
November 1967

Congratulations / High 'n' Dry
DB 8376
March 1968

**I'll Love You Forever Today /
   Girl, You'll Be A Woman Soon**
DB 8437
June 1968

Marianne / Mr Nice
DB 8476
September 1968

**Don't Forget To Catch Me /
   What's More (I Don't Need Her)**
DB 8503
November 1968

**Good Times (Better Times) /
   Occasional Rain**
DB 8548
February 1969

Big Ship / She's Leaving You
DB 8581
May 1969

Throw Down A Line (*with Hank Marvin*) **/
   Reflections**
DB 8615
September 1969

With The Eyes Of A Child / So Long
DB 8648
November 1969

**The Joy Of Living /
   Leave My Woman Alone / Boogatoo**
DB 8657
February 1970

**Goodbye Sam, Hello Samantha /
   You Can Never Tell**
DB 8685
June 1970

**I Ain't Got Time Anymore /
   Monday Comes Too Soon**
DB 8708
August 1970

Sunny Honey Girl / Don't Move Away (*with
   Olivia Newton-John*) **/
   I Was Only Fooling Myself**
DB 8747
January 1971

**Silvery Rain / Annabella Umbrella /
   Time Flies**
DB 8774
April 1971

Flying Machine / Pigeon
DB 8797
July 1971

**Sing A Song Of Freedom /
   A Thousand Conversations**
DB 8836
November 1971

Jesus / Mr Cloud
DB 8864
March 1972

Living In Harmony / Empty Chairs
DB 8917
August 1972

A Brand New Song / The Old Accordion
DB 8957
December 1972

**Power To All Our Friends /
    Come Back Billie Jo**
EMI 2012
March 1973

**Help It Along / Tomorrow Rising /
    Days Of Love / Ashes To Ashes**
EMI 2022
May 1973

Take Me High / Celestial Houses
EMI 2088
November 1973

(You Keep Me) Hangin' On / Love Is Here
EMI 2150
May 1974

**It's Only Me You've Left Behind /
    You're The One**
EMI 2279
March 1975

**(There's A) Honky Tonk Angel (Who Will
    Take Me Back In) / Wouldn't You Know It**
EMI 2344
September 1975

Miss You Nights / Love Is Enough
EMI 2376
February 1976

Devil Woman / Love On
EMI 2485
May 1976

**I Can't Ask For Anything More Than You /
    Junior Cowboy**
EMI 2499
August 1976

Hey Mr Dream Maker / No One Waits
EMI 2559
November 1976

My Kinda Life / Nothing Left For Me To Say
EMI 2584
February 1977

**When Two Worlds Drift Apart /
    That's Why I Love You**
EMI 2663
June 1977

Yes! He Lives / Good On The Sally Army
EMI 2730
January 1978

Please Remember Me / Please Don't Tease
EMI 2832
July 1978

**Can't Take The Hurt Anymore /
    Needing A Friend**
EMI 2885
November 1978

Green Light / Imagine Love
EMI 2920
March 1979

We Don't Talk Anymore / Count Me Out
EMI 2675
July 1979

Hot Shot / Walking In The Light
EMI 5003
November 1979

Carrie / Moving In
EMI 5006
February 1980

Dreamin' / Dynamite
EMI 5095
August 1980

Suddenly (*with Olivia Newton-John*) **/ You
    Made Me Love You** (*Olivia Newton-John*)
JET 7002
October 1980

A Little In Love / Keep On Looking
EMI 5123
January 1981

Wired For Sound / Hold On
EMI 5221
August 1981

Daddy's Home / Shakin' All Over
EMI 5251
November 1981

The Only Way Out / Under The Influence
EMI 5318
July 1982

Where Do We Go From Here? / Discovering
EMI 5341
September 1982

**Little Town / Love And A Helping Hand /
    You, Me And Jesus**
EMI 5348
November 1982

She Means Nothing To Me (*with Phil
    Everly*) / **A Man And A Woman** (*Phil
    Everly*)
Capitol CL 276
January 1983

True Love Ways / Galadriel
EMI 5385
April 1983

Drifting (*with Sheila Walsh*) / **It's Lonely
    When The Lights Go Out** (*Sheila Walsh*)
DJM SHEIL 1
May 1983

Drifting (*with Sheila Walsh*) / **It's Lonely
    When The Lights Go Out** (*Sheila Walsh*)
DJM SHEIL 100 – 12″ single
May 1983

Never Say Die / Lucille
EMI 5415
August 1983

Never Say Die / Lucille
EMI 12EMI 5415 – 12″ single
August 1983

**Please Don't Fall In Love /
    Too Close To Heaven**
EMI 5437
November 1983

Baby You're Dynamite / Ocean Deep
EMI 5457
March 1984

Two To The Power (*with Janet Jackson*) /
    Rock And Roll (*Janet Jackson*)
A & M AM 210
September 1984

Two To The Power (*with Janet Jackson*) /
    **Rock And Roll / Don't Mess Up This Good
    Thing** (*Janet Jackson*)
A & M AMX 210 – 12″ single
September 1984

Shooting From The Heart / Small World
Rich 1
October 1984

Shooting From The Heart / Small World
RICHP 1 – picture disc
November 1984

Heart User / I Will Follow You
Rich 2
January 1985

She's So Beautiful / She's So Beautiful
    (*instrumental*)
EMI 5531
September 1985

It's In Every One Of Us / Alone
    (*instrumental*)
EMI 5537
November 1985

**It's In Every One Of Us / It's In Every One
    Of Us** (*instrumental*) / **Alone**
EMI 12EMI 5537 – 12″ single
November 1985

Living Doll (*with The Young Ones*) / **Happy**
WEA YZ65
March 1986

Living Doll (*with The Young Ones*) / **Happy /
    Disco Funk Get Up Get Down**
WEA YZ65T – 12″ single
March 1986

Born To Rock 'n' Roll / Law Of The Universe
EMI 5545
May 1986

Born To Rock 'n' Roll / Law Of The Universe
EMI 12EMI 5545 – 12″ single
May 1986

All I Ask Of You (*with Sarah Brightman*) **/**
Phantom Of The Opera Overture
Polydor POSP 802
September 1986

All I Ask Of You (*with Sarah Brightman*) **/**
Phantom Of The Opera Overture /
Only You
Polydor POSPX 802 – 12″ single
September 1986

Slow Rivers (*with Elton John*) **/**
Billy And The Kids (*Elton John*)
ROCKET EJS 13
November 1986

Slow Rivers (*with Elton John*) **/ Billy And**
The Kids / Lord Of The Flies (*Elton John*)
ROCKET EJS 13–12 – 12″ single
November 1986

My Pretty One / Love Ya
EM 4
June 1987

My Pretty One / Love Ya / Under The Gun
12EM 4 – 12″ single
June 1987

My Pretty One / Love Ya
EMG 4 – gatefold sleeve
June 1987

My Pretty One / Love Ya / Under The Gun
12EMP 4 – 12″ single with poster
June 1987

Some People / One Time Lover Man
EM 18
August 1987

Some People / One Time Lover Man
12EM 18 – 12″ single
August 1987

Some People / One Time Lover Man
EMG 18 – gatefold sleeve
August 1987

Some People / One Time Lover Man
EMP 18 – picture disc
August 1987

Remember Me / Another Christmas Day
EM 31
October 1987

Remember Me / Another Christmas Day /
Brave New World
12EM 31 – 12″ single
October 1987

Remember Me / Another Christmas Day /
Some People
CDEM 31 – CD single
October 1987

Remember Me / Another Christmas Day /
Brave New World
12EMP 31 – special 12″ single
October 1987

Two Hearts / Yesterday, Today, Forever
EM 42
February 1988

Two Hearts / Yesterday, Today, Forever /
Wild Geese
12EM 42 – 12″ single
February 1988

Two Hearts / Yesterday, Today, Forever /
Wild Geese
12EMG 42 – 12″ gatefold single with Valentine's
card
February 1988

Mistletoe And Wine / Marmaduke
EM 78
November 1988

**Mistletoe And Wine / Marmaduke /
    Little Town**
12EM 78 – 12″ single
November 1988

**Mistletoe And Wine / Marmaduke /
    Little Town / La Gonave**
CDEM 78 – CD single with Christmas card
November 1988

**Mistletoe And Wine / Marmaduke /
    True Love Ways**
EMS 78 – Special 7″
November 1988

**Mistletoe And Wine / Marmaduke /
    Little Town**
12EMX 78 – 12″ single with Advent calendar
November 1988

Mistletoe And Wine / Marmaduke
EMP 78 – 7″ Poster bag with calendar
November 1988

The Best Of Me / Move It / Lindsay Jane
EM 92
May 1989

**The Best Of Me / Move It / Lindsay Jane /
    High Class Baby**
12EM 92 – 12″ single
May 1989

**I Just Don't Have The Heart /
    Wide Open Space**
EM 101
August 1989

**I Just Don't Have The Heart /
    Wide Open Space / I Just Don't Have
    The Heart** (*instrumental*)
12EM 101 – 12″ single
August 1989

**I Just Don't Have The Heart /
    Wide Open Space / I Just Don't Have
    The Heart** (*instrumental*)
12EMP 101 – 12″ single with poster
August 1989

**I Just Don't Have The Heart /
    Wide Open Space / I Just Don't Have
    The Heart** (*instrumental*)
CDEM 101 – CD single
August 1989

**I Just Don't Have The Heart /
    Wide Open Space / I Just Don't Have
    The Heart** (*instrumental*)
TCEM 101 – Cassette single
August 1989

Lean On You / Hey Mister
EM 105
October 1989

Lean On You / Hey Mister / Lean On You
    (*extended mix*)
12EM 105 – 12″ single
October 1989

Lean On You / Hey Mister / Lean On You
    (*extended mix*)
EMPD 105 – 7″ picture disc
October 1989

Lean On You / Hey Mister / Lean On You
    (*extended mix*)
CDEM 105 – CD single
October 1989

Lean On You / Hey Mister / Lean On You
    (*extended mix*)
TCEM 105 – Cassette single
October 1989

Stronger Than That / Joanna
EM 129
February 1990

Stronger Than That / Joanna
12EM 129 – 12″ single
February 1990

Stronger Than That / Joanna
12EMP 129 – 12″ poster bag
February 1990

Stronger Than That / Joanna
CDEM 129 – CD single
February 1990

Stronger Than That / Joanna
TCEM 129 – Cassette single
February 1990

Stronger Than That / Joanna
EMS 129 – Postcard pack
February 1990

Silhouettes / The Winner
EM 152
August 1990

Silhouettes / The Winner
EMS 152 – Special package including free print
August 1990

**Silhouettes / The Winner /
All The Time You Need**
12EM 152 – 12″ single
August 1990

**Silhouettes / The Winner /
All The Time You Need**
CDEM 152 – CD single
August 1990

**Silhouettes / The Winner /
All The Time You Need**
TCEM 152 – Cassette single
August 1990

From A Distance / Lindsay Jane II
EM 155
October 1990

**From A Distance / I Could Easily Fall
(In Love With You)**
EMPD 155 – Limited edition 7″ picture disc
featuring alternative B-side
October 1990

**From A Distance / Lindsay Jane II /
Wired For Sound**
12EM 155 – 12″ single
October 1990

**From A Distance / Lindsay Jane II /
Wired For Sound**
12EMP 155 – 12″ single poster bag
October 1990

**From A Distance / Lindsay Jane II /
Wired For Sound**
CDEM 155 – CD single
October 1990

From A Distance / Lindsay Jane II
TCEM 155 – Cassette single
October 1990

Saviour's Day / The 'Oh Boy' Medley
XMAS 90
November 1990

Saviour's Day / The 'Oh Boy' Medley
XMASP 90 – Decade pack includes five photos
from five decades
November 1990

**Saviour's Day / The 'Oh Boy' Medley /
Where You Are**
12XMAS 90 – 12″ single
November 1990

Saviour's Day / The 'Oh Boy' Medley
TCXMAS 90 – Cassette single
November 1990

**Saviour's Day / The 'Oh Boy' Medley /
Where You Are**
CDXMAS 90 – CD single
November 1990

Extended Play

Serious Charge
SEG 7895
May 1959
Living Doll / No Turning Back / Mad About You / Chinchilla (*Shadows*)

Cliff No. 1
SEG 7903 / ESG 7754
June 1959
Apron Strings / My Babe / Down The Line / I Gotta Feeling / Baby I Don't Care / Jet Black (*Shadows*)

Cliff No. 2
SEG 7910 / ESG 7769
July 1959
Donna / Move It / Ready Teddy / Too Much / Don't Bug Me Baby

Expresso Bongo
SEG 7971 / ESG 7783
January 1960
Love / A Voice In The Wilderness / The Shrine On The Second Floor / Bongo Blues (*Shadows*)

Cliff Sings No. 1
SEG 7979 / ESG 7788
February 1960
Here Comes Summer / I Gotta Know / Blue Suede Shoes / The Snake And The Bookworm

Cliff Sings No. 2
SEG 7987 / ESG 7794
March 1960
Twenty Flight Rock / Pointed Toe Shoes / Mean Woman Blues / I'm Walkin'

Cliff Sings No. 3
SEG 8005 / ESG 7808
June 1960
I'll String Along With You / Embraceable You / As Time Goes By / The Touch Of Your Lips

Cliff Sings No. 4
SEG 8021 / ESG 7816
September 1960
I Don't Know Why (I Just Do) / Little Things Mean A Lot / Somewhere Along The Way / That's My Desire

Cliff's Silver Discs
SEG 8050
December 1960
Please Don't Tease / Fall In Love With You / Nine
Times Out Of Ten / Travellin' Light

Me And My Shadows No. 1
SEG 8065 / ESG 7837
February 1961
I'm Gonna Get You / You And I / I Cannot Find A
True Love / Evergreen Tree / She's Gone

Me And My Shadows No. 2
SEG 8071 / ESG 7481
March 1961
Left Out Again / You're Just The One To Do It /
Lamp Of Love / Choppin' And Changin' /
We Have It Made

Me And My Shadows No. 3
SEG 8078 / ESG 7843
April 1961
Tell Me / Gee Whiz It's You / I'm Willing To
Learn / I Love You So / I Don't Know

Listen To Cliff
SEG 8105 / ESG 7858
October 1961
What'd I Say / True Love Will Come To You /
Blue Moon / Lover

Dream
SEG 8119 / ESG 7867
November 1961
Dream / All I Do Is Dream Of You / I'll See You In
My Dreams / When I Grow Too Old To Dream

Listen to Cliff No. 2
SEG 8126 / ESG 7870
December 1961
Unchained Melody / First Lesson In Love / Idle
Gossip / Almost Like Being In Love / Beat Out
Dat Rhythm On A Drum

Cliff's Hit Parade
SEG 8133
February 1962
I Love You / Theme For A Dream / A Girl Like
You / When The Girl In Your Arms (Is The Girl
In Your Heart)

Cliff Richard No. 1
SEG 8151
April 1962
Forty Days / Catch Me / How Wonderful To
Know / Tough Enough

Hits From 'The Young Ones'
SEG 8159
May 1962
The Young Ones / Got A Funny Feeling / Lessons
   In Love / We Say Yeah

Cliff Richard No. 2
SEG 8168
June 1962
Fifty Tears For Every Kiss / The Night Is So
   Lonely / Poor Boy / Y'Arriva

Cliff's Hits
SEG 8203
November 1962
It'll Be Me / Since I Lost You / Do You Want To
   Dance / I'm Looking Out The Window

Time For Cliff And The Shadows
SEG 8228 / ESG 7887
March 1963
So I've Been Told / I'm Walkin' The Blues / When
   My Dreamboat Comes Home / Blueberry Hill /
   You Don't Know

Holiday Carnival
SEG 8246 / ESG 7892
May 1963
Carnival / Moonlight Bay / Some Of These Days /
   For You For Me

Hits From 'Summer Holiday'
SEG 8250 / ESG 7896
June 1963
Summer Holiday / The Next Time / Dancing
   Shoes / Bachelor Boy

More Hits From 'Summer Holiday'
SEG 8263 / ESG 7898
September 1963
Seven Days To A Holiday / Stranger In Town /
   Really Waltzing / All At Once

Cliff's Lucky Lips
SEG 8269
October 1963
It's All In The Game / Your Eyes Tell On You /
   Lucky Lips / I Wonder

Love Songs
SEG 8272 / ESG 7900
November 1963
I'm In The Mood For Love / Secret Love / Love
   Letters / I Only Have Eyes For You

When In France
SEG 8290
February 1964
La Mer / Boum / J'Attendrai / C'est Si Bon

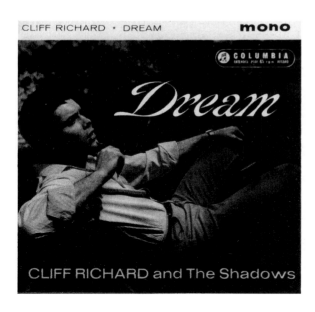

Cliff Sings Don't Talk To Him
SEG 8299
March 1964
Don't Talk To Him / Say You're Mine / Spanish
    Harlem / Who Are We To Say / Falling In Love
    With Love

Cliff's Palladium Successes
SEG 8320
May 1964
I'm The Lonely One / Watch What You Do With
    My Baby / Perhaps Perhaps Perhaps / Frenesi

Wonderful Life No. 1
SEG 8338 / ESG 7902
August 1964
Wonderful Life / Do You Remember / What've I
    Gotta Do / Walkin' (*Shadows*)

A Forever Kind Of Love
SEG 8347
September 1964
A Forever Kind Of Love / It's Wonderful To Be
    Young / Constantly / True True Lovin'

Wonderful Life No. 2
SEG 8354 / ESG 7903
October 1964
A Matter Of Moments / Girl In Every Port /
    A Little Imagination / In The Stars

Hits From Wonderful Life
SEG 8376 / ESG 7906
December 1964
On The Beach / We Love A Movie / Home / All
    Kinds Of People

Why Don't They Understand
SEG 8384
February 1965
Why Don't They Understand / Where The Four
    Winds Blow / The Twelfth Of Never / I'm
    Afraid To Go Home

**Cliff's Hits From Aladdin And His
    Wonderful Lamp**
SEG 8395
March 1965
Havin' Fun / Evening Comes / Friends / I Could
    Easily Fall (In Love With You)

Look In My Eyes Maria
SEG 8405
May 1965
Look In My Eyes Maria / Where Is Your Heart /
    Maria / If I Give My Heart To You

Angel
SEG 8444
September 1965
Angel / I Only Came To Say Goodbye / On My
    Word / The Minute You're Gone

Take Four
SEG 8450
October 1965
Boom Boom / My Heart Is An Open Book / Lies
    And Kisses / Sweet And Gentle

Wind Me Up
SEG 8474
February 1966
Wind Me Up / The Night / The Time In Between /
    Look Before You Love

Hits From 'When In Rome'
SEG 8478
April 1966
Come Prima (For The First Time) / Nel Blu Di
    Pinto Di Blu (Volare) / Dicitencello Vuie (Just
    Say I Love Her) / Arrivederci Roma

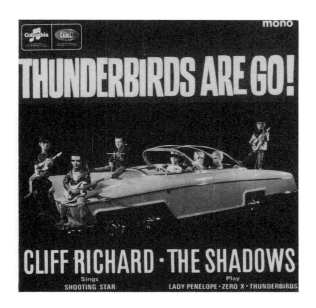

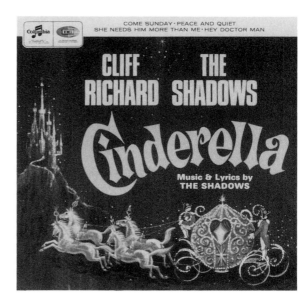

Love Is Forever
SEG 8488
April 1966
My Colouring Book / Fly Me To The Moon /
    Someday / Everyone Needs Someone To Love

Thunderbirds Are Go
SEG 8510
December 1966
Shooting Star / Lady Penelope (*Shadows*) /
    Thunderbirds Theme (*Shadows*) / Zero X
    Theme (*Shadows*)

La La La La La
SEG 8517
December 1966
La La La La La / Solitary Man (*Shadows*) /
    Things We Said Today / Never Knew What
    Love Could Do

Cinderella
SEG 8527
May 1967
Come Sunday / Peace And Quiet / She Needs
    Him More Than Me / Hey Doctor Man

Carol Singers
SEG 8533
November 1967
God Rest Ye Merry Gentlemen / In The Bleak
    Midwinter / Unto Us A Boy Is Born / While
    Shepherds Watched / O Little Town Of
    Bethlehem

Congratulations
SEG 8540
April 1968
Congratulations / Wonderful World / Do You
    Remember / High 'n' Dry / The Sound Of The
    Candyman's Trumpet / Little Rag Doll

Albums

Cliff
SX 1147
April 1959
Apron Strings / My Babe / Down The Line / I Got A Feeling / Jet Black (*Drifters*) / Baby I Don't Care / Donna / Move It / Ready Teddy / Too Much / Don't Bug Me Baby / Driftin' (*Drifters*) / That'll Be The Day / Be Bop A Lula (*Drifters*) / Danny / Whole Lotta Shakin' Goin' On

Cliff Sings
SX 1192
November 1959
Blue Suede Shoes / The Snake And The Bookworm / I Gotta Know / Here Comes Summer / I'll String Along With You / Embraceable You / As Time Goes By / The Touch Of Your Lips / Twenty Flight Rock / Pointed Toe Shoes / Mean Woman Blues / I'm Walking / I Don't Know Why / Little Things Mean A Lot / Somewhere Along The Way / That's My Desire

Me And My Shadows
SX 1261 / SCX 3330
October 1960
I'm Gonna Get You / You And I / I Cannot Find A True Love / Evergreen Tree / She's Gone / Left Out Again / You're Just The One To Do It / Lamp Of Love / Choppin' And Changin' / We Have It Made / Tell Me / Gee Whiz It's You / I Love You So / I'm Willing To Learn / I Don't Know / Working After School

Listen To Cliff
SX 1320 / SCX 3375
May 1961
What'd I Say / Blue Moon / True Love Will Come To You / Lover / Unchained Melody / Idle Gossip / First Lesson In Love / Almost Like Being In Love / Beat Out Dat Rhythm On A Drum / Memories Linger On / Temptation / I Live For You / Sentimental Journey / I Want You To Know / We Kiss In A Shadow / It's You

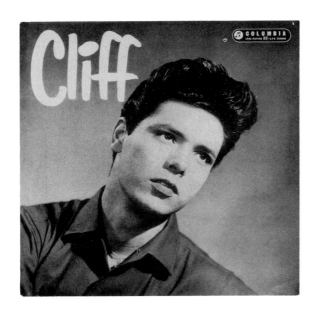

21 Today

SX 1368 / SCX 3409

October 1961

Happy Birthday To You / Forty Days / Catch Me / How Wonderful To Know / Tough Enough / Fifty Tears For Every Kiss / The Night Is So Lonely / Poor Boy / Y'Arriva / Outsider / Tea For Two / To Prove My Love For You / Without You / A Mighty Lonely Man / My Blue Heaven / Shame On You

The Young Ones

SX 1384 / SCX 3397

December 1961

Friday Night / Got A Funny Feeling / Peace Pipe (*Shadows*) / Nothing's Impossible / The Young Ones / All For One / Lessons In Love / No One For Me But Nicki / What Do You Know We've Got A Show – Vaudeville Routine / When The Girl In Your Arms (Is The Girl In Your Heart) / Just Dance / Mood Mambo / The Savage (*Shadows*) / We Say Yeah

32 Minutes And 17 Seconds With Cliff Richard

SX 1431 / SCX 3436

October 1962

It'll Be Me / So I've Been Told / How Long Is Forever / I'm Walkin' The Blues / Turn

Around / Blueberry Hill / Let's Make A Memory / When My Dreamboat Comes Home / I'm On My Way / Spanish Harlem / You Don't Know / Falling In Love With Love / Who Are We To Say / I Wake Up Cryin'

Summer Holiday

SX 1472 / SCX 3462

January 1963

Seven Days To A Holiday / Summer Holiday / Let Us Take You For A Ride / Les Girls (*Shadows*) / Round And Round (*Shadows*) / Foot Tapper (*Shadows*) / Stranger In Town / Orlando's Mime / Bachelor Boy / A Swingin' Affair / Really Waltzing / All At Once / Dancing Shoes / Yugoslav Wedding / The Next Time / Big News

Cliff's Hit Album

SX 1512 / SCX 1512

July 1963

Move It / Living Doll / Travellin' Light / A Voice In The Wilderness / Fall In Love With You / Please Don't Tease / Nine Times Out Of Ten / I Love You / Theme For A Dream / A Girl Like You / When The Girl In Your Arms / The Young Ones / I'm Looking Out The Window / Do You Wanna Dance

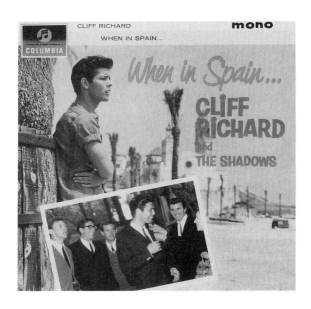

When In Spain
SX 1541/SCX 3488
September 1963
Perfidia/Amor, Amor, Amor/Frenesi/You
Belong To My Heart/Vaya Con Dios/Sweet
And Gentle/Maria No Mas/Kiss/Perhaps
Perhaps Perhaps/Magic Is The Moonlight/
Carnival/Sway

Wonderful Life
SX 1628/SCX 3515
July 1964
Wonderful Life/A Girl In Every Port/Walkin'
(*Shadows*)/A Little Imagination/Home/On
The Beach/In The Stars/We Love A Movie/
Do You Remember/What've I Gotta Do/
Theme For Young Lovers (*Shadows*)/All
Kinds Of People/A Matter Of Moments/
Youth And Experience

Aladdin And His Wonderful Lamp
SX 1676/SCX 3522
December 1964
Emperor Theme (*Orchestra*)/Chinese Street
Scene (*Orchestra*)/Me Oh My (*Shadows*)/I
Could Easily Fall (In Love With You)/Little
Princess (*Shadows*)/This Was My Special
Day/I'm In Love With You/There's Gotta Be
A Way/Ballet: (Rubies, Emeralds, Sapphires,
Diamonds) (*Orchestra*)/Dance Of The
Warriors (*Orchestra*)/Friends/Dragon
Dance (*Orchestra*)/Genie With The Light
Brown Lamp (*Shadows*)/Make Ev'ry Day A
Carnival Day/Widow Twankey's Song
(*Orchestra*)/I'm Feeling Oh So Lonely
(*Orchestra*)/I've Said Too Many Things/
Evening Comes/Havin' Fun

Cliff Richard
SX 1709/SCX 3456
April 1965
Angel/Sway/I Only Came To Say Goodbye/
Take Special Care/Magic Is The Moonlight/
House Without Windows/Razzle Dazzle/I
Don't Wanna Love You/It's Not For Me To
Say/You Belong To My Heart/Again/
Perfidia/Kiss/Reelin' And Rockin'

More Hits By Cliff
SX 1737/SCX 3555
July 1965
It'll Be Me/The Next Time/Bachelor Boy/
Summer Holiday/Dancing Shoes/Lucky
Lips/It's All In The Game/Don't Talk To
Him/I'm The Lonely One/Constantly/On the
Beach/A Matter Of Moments/The Twelfth Of
Never/I Could Easily Fall (In Love With You)

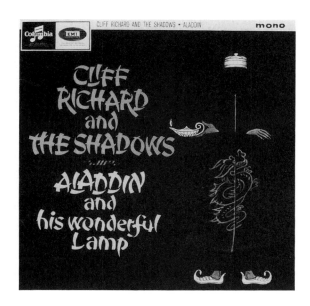

When In Rome
SX 1762
August 1965
Come Prima / Volare / Autumn Concerto / The
Questions / Maria's Her Name / Don't Talk To
Him / Just Say I Love Her / Arrivederci Roma /
Carina / A Little Grain Of Sand / House
Without Windows / Che Cosa Del Farai Mia
Amour / Tell Me You're Mine

Love Is Forever
SX 1769 / SCX 3569
November 1965
Everyone Needs Someone To Love / Long Ago
And Far Away / All Of A Sudden My Heart
Sings / Have I Told You Lately That I Love
You / Fly Me To The Moon / A Summer Place / I
Found A Rose / My Foolish Heart / Through
The Eye Of A Needle / My Colouring Book / I
Walk Alone / Someday (You'll Want Me To
Love You) / Paradise Lost / Look Homeward
Angel

Kinda Latin
SX 6039 / SCX 6039
May 1966
Blame It On The Bossa Nova / Blowing In The
Wind / Quiet Nights Of Quiet Stars / Eso Beso /
The Girl From Ipanema / One Note Samba /

Fly Me To The Moon / Our Day Will Come /
Quando, Quando, Quando / Come Closer To
Me / Meditation / Concrete And Clay

Finders Keepers
SX 6079 / SCX 6079
December 1966
Finders Keepers / Time Drags By /
Washerwoman / La La La Song / My Way / Oh
Señorita / Spanish Music / Fiesta (*Shadows*) /
This Day / Paella / Finders Keepers / My Way /
Paella / Fiesta (*Shadows*) / Run To The Door /
Where Did The Summer Go / Into Each Life
Some Rain Must Fall

Cinderella
SX 6103 / SCX 6103
January 1967
Welcome To Stoneybroke / Why Wasn't I Born
Rich / Peace And Quiet / The Flyder And The
Spy (*Shadows*) / Poverty / The Hunt / In The
Country / Come Sunday / Dare I Love Him Like
I Do / If Our Dreams Come True / Autumn /
The King's Place / Peace And Quiet / She
Needs Him More Than Me / Hey Doctor Man

Don't Stop Me Now

SX 6133 / SCX 6133

April 1967

Shout / One Fine Day / I'll Be Back / Heartbeat / I Saw Her Standing There / Hang On To A Dream / You Gotta Tell Me / Homeward Bound / Good Golly Miss Molly / Don't Make Promises / Move It / Don't / Dizzy Miss Lizzy / Baby It's You / My Babe / Save The Last Dance For Me

Good News

SX 6167 / SCX 6167

October 1967

Good News / It Is No Secret / We Shall Be Changed / 23rd Psalm / Go Where I Send Thee / What A Friend We Have In Jesus / All Glory Laud And Honour / Just A Closer Walk With Thee / The King Of Love My Shepherd Is / Mary What You Gonna Name That Pretty Little Baby / When I Survey The Wondrous Cross / Take My Hand Precious Lord / Get On Board Little Children / May The Good Lord Bless And Keep You

Cliff In Japan

SX 6244 / SCX 6244

May 1968

Shout / I'll Come Running / The Minute You're Gone / On The Beach / Hang On To A Dream / Spanish Harlem / Finders Keepers / Visions / Evergreen Tree / What'd I Say / Dynamite / Medley: Let's Make A Memory – The Young Ones – Lucky Lips – Summer Holiday – We Say Yeah

Two A Penny

SX 6262 / SCX 6262

August 1968

Two A Penny / I'll Love You Forever Today / Questions / Long Is The Night (*instrumental*) / Lonely Girl / And Me (I'm On The Outside Now) / Daybreak (*instrumental*) / Twist And Shout / Celeste (*instrumental*) / Wake Up Wake Up / Cloudy / Red Rubber Ball / Close To Cathy / Rattler

Established 1958

SX 6282 / SCX 6282

September 1968

Don't Forget To Catch Me / Voyage To The Bottom Of The Bath (*Shadows*) / Not The Way It Should Be / Poem / The Dreams I Dream / The Average Life Of A Daily Man (*Shadows*) / Somewhere By The Sea / Banana Man (*Shadows*) / Girl On The Bus / The Magical Mrs Clamps (*Shadows*) / Ooh La La / Here I Go Again Loving You (*Shadows*) / What's Behind The Eyes Of Mary / Maggie's Samba (*Shadows*)

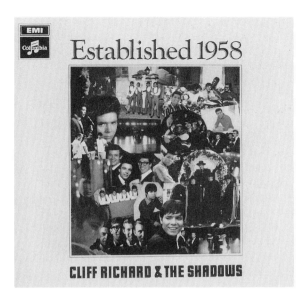

The Best Of Cliff
SX 6343 / SCX 6343
June 1969
The Minute You're Gone / On My Word / The
    Time In Between / Wind Me Up (Let Me Go) /
    Blue Turns To Grey / Visions / Time Drags By /
    In The Country / It's All Over / I'll Come
    Running / The Day I Met Marie / All My Love /
    Congratulations / Girl You'll Be A Woman
    Soon

Sincerely Cliff Richard
SCX 6357
October 1969
In The Past / Always / Will You Love Me
    Tomorrow / You'll Want Me / I'm Not Getting
    Married / Time / For Emily Whenever I May
    Find Her / Baby I Could Be So Good At
    Loving You / Sam / London's Not Too Far /
    Take Action / Take Good Care Of Her /
    When I Find You / Punch And Judy

Cliff Live At The Talk Of The Town
SRS 5031
July 1970
Introduction / Congratulations / Shout / All My
    Love / Ain't Nothing But A House Party /
    Something Good / If Ever I Should Leave You /
    Girl You'll Be A Woman Soon / Hank's
    Medley / London's Not Too Far / The Dreams
    That I Dream / The Day I Met Marie / La La La
    La La / A Taste Of Honey / The Lady Came
    From Baltimore / When I'm 64 / What's More I
    Don't Need Her / Bows And Fanfare /
    Congratulations / Visions / Finale:
    Congratulations

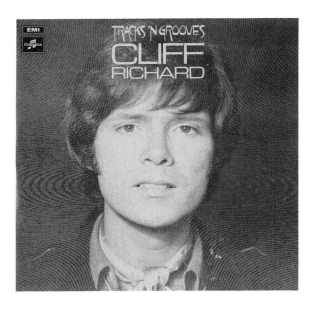

About That Man
SCX 6408
October 1970
The Birth Of John The Baptist / Sweet Little
   Jesus Boy / The Visit Of The Wise Men And
   The Escape Into Egypt / John The Baptist
   Points Out Jesus / Jesus Recruits His Helpers
   And Heals The Sick / Where Is That Man /
   Jesus Addresses The Crowd On The Hillside /
   Can It Be True / Jesus Is Betrayed And
   Arrested / The Trial Of Jesus / His Execution
   And Death / The First Easter – The Empty
   Tomb / Reflections

His Land
SCX 6443
November 1970
Ezekiel's Vision / Dry Bones / His Land /
   Jerusalem Jerusalem / The New 23rd / His
   Land / Hava Nagila / Over In Bethlehem / Keep
   Me Where Love Is / He's Everything To Me /
   Narration And Hallelujah Chorus

Tracks 'n' Grooves
SCX 6435
November 1970
Early In The Morning / As I Walk Into The
   Morning Of Your Life / Love Truth And Emily
   Stone / My Head Goes Around / Put My Mind
   At Ease / Abraham, Martin And John / The Girl
   Can't Help It / Bang Bang (My Baby Shot Me

Down) / I'll Make It All Up To You / I'd Just Be
Fool Enough / Don't Let Tonight Ever End /
What A Silly Thing To Do / Your Heart's Not
In Your Love / Don't Ask Me To Be Friends /
Are You Only Fooling Me

The Best Of Cliff Volume Two
SXX 6519
November 1972
Goodbye Sam, Hello Samantha / Marianne /
   Throw Down A Line / Jesus / Sunny Honey
   Girl / I Ain't Got Time Anymore / Flying
   Machine / Sing A Song Of Freedom / With The
   Eyes Of A Child / Good Times / I'll Love You
   Forever Today / The Joy Of Living / Silvery
   Rain / Big Ship

Take Me High
EMI EMC 3016
December 1973
It's Only Money / Midnight Blue / Hover / Why /
   Life / Driving / The Game / Brumburger Duet /
   Take Me High / The Anti-Brotherhood Of
   Man / Winning / Driving / Join The Band / The
   Word Is Love / Brumburger (Finale)

Help It Along
EMI EMA 768
June 1974
Day By Day / Celestial Houses / Jesus / Silvery Rain / Jesus Loves You / Fire And Rain / Yesterday Today Forever / Mr Businessman / Help It Along / Amazing Grace / Higher Ground / Sing A Song Of Freedom

The 31st Of February Street
EMI EMC 3048
November 1974
31st Of February Street Opening / Give Me Back That Old Familiar Feeling / The Leaving / Travellin' Light / There You Go Again / Nothing To Remind Me / Our Love Could Be So Real / No Matter What / Fireside Song / Going Away / Long Long Time / You Will Never Know / The Singer / 31st Of February Street Closing

I'm Nearly Famous
EMI EMC 3122
May 1976
I Can't Ask For Any More Than You / It's No Use Pretending / I'm Nearly Famous / Lovers / Junior Cowboy / Miss You Nights / I Wish You'd Change Your Mind / Devil Woman / Such Is The Mystery / You've Got To Give Me All Your Lovin' / Alright It's Alright

Every Face Tells A Story
EMI EMC 3172
March 1977
My Kinda Life / Must Be Love / When Two Worlds Drift Apart / You Got Me Wondering / Every Face Tells A Story (It Never Tells A Lie) / Try A Smile / Hey Mr Dream Maker / Give Me Love Your Way / Don't Turn The Light Out / It'll Be Me Babe / Spider Man

40 Golden Greats
EMI EMTVS 6 / TCEMTVS 6 / CDEMTVS 6
September 1977
Move It / Living Doll / Travellin' Light / Fall In Love With You / Please Don't Tease / Nine Times Out Of Ten / Theme For A Dream / Gee Whiz It's You / When The Girl In Your Arms (Is The Girl In Your Heart) / A Girl Like You / The Young Ones / Do You Wanna Dance / I'm Looking Out The Window / It'll Be Me / Bachelor Boy / The Next Time / Summer Holiday / Lucky Lips / It's All In The Game / Don't Talk To Him / Constantly / On The Beach / I Could Easily Fall (In Love With You) / The Minute You're Gone / Wind Me Up (Let Me Go) / Visions / Blue Turns To Grey / In The Country / The Day I Met Marie / All My Love / Congratulations / Throw Down A Line / Goodbye Sam, Hello Samantha / Sing A Song Of Freedom / Power To All Our Friends / (You

Keep Me) Hangin' On / Miss You Nights / Devil
Woman / I Can't Ask For Any More Than You /
My Kinda Life

Small Corners
EMI EMC 3219
February 1978
Why Should The Devil Have All The Good
   Music / I Love / Why Me Lord / I've Got News
   For You / Hey Watcha Say / I Wish We'd All
   Been Ready / Joseph / Good On The Sally
   Army / Goin' Home / Up In Canada / Yes He
   Lives / When I Survey The Wondrous Cross

Green Light
EMI EMC 3231
September 1978
Green Light / Under Lock And Key / She's A
   Gypsy / Count Me Out / Please Remember Me /
   Never Even Thought / Free My Soul / Start All
   Over Again / While She's Young / Can't Take
   The Hurt Anymore / Ease Along

Thank You Very Much
EMI EMTV 15
February 1979
The Young Ones / Do You Wanna Dance / The
   Day I Met Marie / Shadoogie (*Shadows*) /
   Atlantis (*Shadows*) / Nivram (*Shadows*) /
   Apache (*Shadows*) / Please Don't Tease / Miss
   You Nights / Move It / Willie And The Hand

Jive / All Shook Up / Devil Woman / Why
Should The Devil Have All The Good Music /
End Of The Show

Rock 'n' Roll Juvenile
EMI EMC 3307 / TCEMC 3307
September 1979
Monday Thru Friday / Doin' Fine / Cities May
   Fall / You Know That I Love You / My Luck
   Won't Change / Rock 'n' Roll Juvenile / Carrie /
   Hot Shot / Language Of Love / We Don't Talk
   Anymore / Sci Fi

I'm No Hero
EMI EMA 796
September 1980
Take Another Look / Anything I Can Do / A Little
   In Love / Here (So Doggone Blue) / Give A
   Little Bit More / In The Night / I'm No Hero /
   Dreamin' / A Heart Will Break / Everyman

Love Songs
EMTV 27 / TCEMTV 27 / CDEMTV 27
July 1981
Miss You Nights / Constantly / Up In The World /
   Carrie / A Voice In The Wilderness / The
   Twelfth Of Never / I Could Easily Fall (In Love
   With You) / The Day I Met Marie / Can't Take
   The Hurt Anymore / A Little In Love / The
   Minute You're Gone / Visions / When Two
   Worlds Drift Apart / The Next Time / It's All In

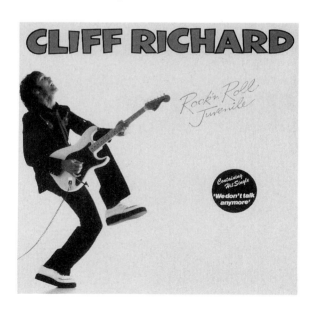

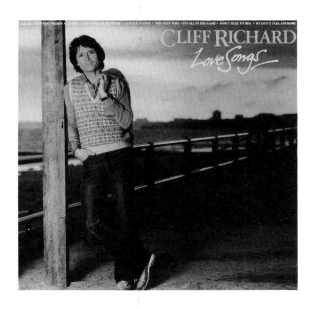

The Game / Don't Talk To Him / When The Girl In Your Arms (Is The Girl In Your Heart) / Theme For A Dream / Fall In Love With You / We Don't Talk Anymore

Wired For Sound
EMC 3377 / TCEMI 5221
September 1981
Wired For Sound / Once In A While / Better Than I Know Myself / Oh No Don't Let Go / 'Cos I Love That Rock 'n' Roll / Broken Doll / Lost In

A Lonely World / Summer Rain / Young Love / Say You Don't Mind / Daddy's Home

Now You See Me . . . Now You Don't
EMC 3415 / TCEMC 3415
August 1982
The Only Way Out / First Date / Thief In The Night / Where Do We Go From Here / Son Of Thunder / Little Town / It Has To Be You It Has To Be Me / The Water Is Wide / Now You See Me Now You Don't / Be In My Heart / Discovering

Dressed For The Occasion
EMC 3432 / TCEMC 3432
May 1983
Green Light / We Don't Talk Anymore / True Love Ways / Softly As I Leave You / Carrie / Miss You Nights / Galadriel / Maybe Someday / Thief In The Night / Up In The World / Treasure Of Love / Devil Woman

Silver
EMC 1077871
October 1983
Silver's Home Tonight / Hold On / Never Say Die (Give A Little Bit More) / Front Page / Ocean Deep / Locked Inside Your Prison / Please Don't Fall In Love / Baby You're Dynamite / The Golden Days Are Over / Love Stealer

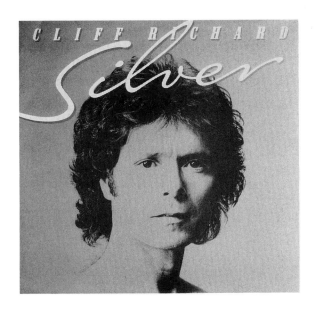

Rock 'n' Roll Silver

Makin' History / Move It / Donna / Teddy Bear /
It'll Be Me / Lucille / Little Bitty Pretty One /
There'll Never Be Anyone Else But You / Be
Bop A Lula / Tutti Frutti

The Rock Connection

Clif2 / TCCLIF 2
November 1984
Heart User / Willie And The Hand Jive / Lovers
And Friends / Never Be Anyone Else But You /

La Gonave / Over You / Shooting From The
Heart / Learning How To Rock 'n' Roll /
Lucille / Be Bop A Lula / Donna / Dynamite /
She Means Nothing To Me / Makin' History

Always Guaranteed

EMD 1004 / TCEMD 1004
September 1987
One Night / Once Upon A Time / Some People /
Forever / Two Hearts / Under Your Spell / This
Time Now / My Pretty One / Remember Me /
Always Guaranteed

Private Collection

CRTV 30 / TCCRTV 30 / CDCRTV 30
November 1988
Some People / Wired For Sound / All I Ask Of
You / Carrie / Remember Me / True Love Ways /
Dreamin' / Green Light / She Means Nothing
To Me / Heart User / A Little In Love / Daddy's
Home / We Don't Talk Anymore / Never Say
Die / The Only Way Out / Suddenly / Slow
Rivers / Please Don't Fall In Love / Little
Town / My Pretty One / Ocean Deep / She's So
Beautiful / Two Hearts / Mistletoe And Wine

Stronger

EMD 1012 / TCEMD 1012 / CDEMD 1012
October 1989
Stronger Than That / Who's In Love / The Best
Of Me / Clear Blue Skies / Keep Me Warm /

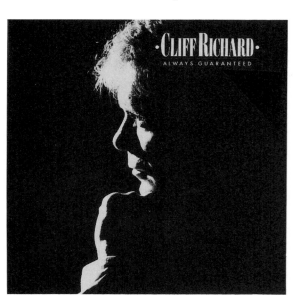

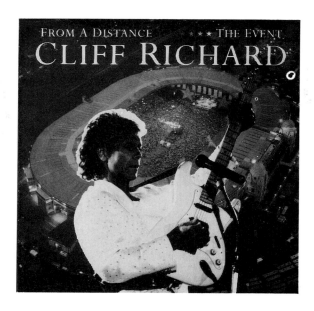

Lean On You / I Just Don't Have The Heart / Joanna / Everybody Knows / Share A Dream / Better Day / Forever You Will Be Mine

The EP Collection – Ballads And Love Songs
SEE 280 / SEEK 280 / SEECD 280
October 1989
Look In My Eyes Maria / If I Give My Heart To You / Maria / Secret Love / Love Letters / I Only Have Eyes For You / All I Do Is Dream Of You / When I Grow Too Old To Dream / My Heart Is An Open Book / Boom Boom (That's How My Heart Beats) / Moonlight Bay / A Forever Kind Of Love / La Mer / J'Attendrai / The Shrine On The Second Floor / Where The Four Winds Blow / Solitary Man / Things We Said Today / Carnival / Little Rag Doll

From A Distance – The Event
CRTV 31 / TCCRTV 31 / CDCRTV 31
November 1990
Oh Boy Medley / Zing Went The Strings Of My Heart (*Dallas Boys*) / Always / When (*Kalin Twins*) / The Glory Of Love / Hoots Mon (*Oh Boy Band*) / Don't Look Now (*Vernon Girls*) / The Girl Can't Help It / Sea Cruise / Oh Boy Medley / From A Distance / Some People / We Don't Talk Anymore / Shake Rattle And Roll / Silhouettes / Move It / Summer Holiday / The Young Ones / In The Country / Good Golly Miss Molly / Fighter / Thief In The Night / Share A Dream / All The Time You Need / Saviour's Day

From A Distance – The Event
The Album Box Set / The Cassette Box Set / The CD Box Set
CRTVB 31 / TCCRTVB 31 / CDCRTVB 31
December 1990
Limited edition box set featuring the same tracks as the double album, includes 6 exclusive prints, giant poster-lyrics, plus engraved 7″ single including a cappella version of Miss You Nights.

Song Title Index

The following is a complete song title index of every song Cliff is known to have recorded as listed in the text and session pages of this book. The only titles not recorded by Cliff listed here are certain ones by The Shadows.

The indefinite and definite articles have been included in strict alphabetical order.